DIY Cannabis Business Startup

How to Legally Start, Run, and GROW Your Own Marijuana (Weed, Hemp, Cannabis & CBD) Based Business: A REAL Success Story - Be Your Own BOSS

Table of 2019 Updated State Laws

By

Chris Maxwell

Copyright © 2019 – *Parma Books*

All Rights Reserved.

No part of this publication may be reproduced, stored in a retrieval system or transmitted in any form or by any means, electronic, mechanical, photocopying, recording or otherwise without the proper written consent of the copyright holder, except as permitted under Sections 107 & 108 of the 1976 United States Copyright Act, without the prior written permission of the publisher.

Parma Books publishes its books and guides in a variety of electronic and print formats, Some content that appears in print may not be available in electronic format, and vice versa.

Cover & Book Design by Emily Jacobs

Disclaimer

This book and its contents are intended for educational purposes only.

The information contained in this book should in no way be interpreted as medical, legal, or any other advice concerning the cultivation, sale, or any other use of marijuana.

Although marijuana sale, cultivation, and use are legal in some states and jurisdictions throughout the United States, at the time of publication of this book, it is illegal under federal law as well as in other states and local jurisdictions.

The author and publisher do not advocate violating applicable law.

Because of the variety of laws, regulations, and ordinances concerning marijuana and the fact that the advice and strategies contained herein may not be suitable for your situation, the author and publisher make no expressed or implied warranties and assume no liability whatsoever concerning the accuracy or reliability of the information contained herein.

This includes no expressed warranty of the legality of or likelihood of success in conducting a cannabis-based business.

The author and publisher recommend that anyone reading this book research applicable laws and consult with appropriate licensed professionals and other experts before taking any action in connection with or based on the contents of this book.

Contents

Acknowledgments 1

Introduction 2

Marijuana: A History 10

The Science of Getting High 16

    Sativa vs. Indica 17

    Why Strains Matter 19

    THC and CBD 20

    What Happens When You "Get High" 21

        Absorption 22

        Distribution 22

        Metabolism 22

        Elimination 23

    What it Means to Feel "High" 23

The Commercialization of Marijuana 26

    Marijuana in Pop Culture 27

        The Entertainment Industry 27

        Music 29

        Social Media 30

        Understanding Pop Culture and Weed Usage 31

    New Legislation and Your Business 34

Examining State Laws 38

Weed Laws Listed by State 41

    Alaska 42

    Arizona 43

    Arkansas 44

    California 45

    Colorado 46

    Connecticut 47

    Delaware 48

    Florida 49

    Hawaii 50

    Illinois 51

    Louisiana 52

    Maine 53

    Maryland 54

    Massachusetts 55

    Michigan 56

    Minnesota 57

    Montana 58

    Nevada 59

    New Hampshire 60

New Jersey 61

New Mexico 62

New York 63

North Dakota 64

Ohio 65

Oregon 66

Rhode Island 67

Vermont 68

Washington 69

Why Create New Laws? 69

Reducing Harm 71

Creating Jobs 72

Promote Consumer Safety 73

Medicinal Applications 74

Starting Your Legal Marijuana Business 80

Real Start-Up Costs 81

Find a Niche That Fits a Need 84

Know What the Rules Are 90

Raising Enough Capital 92

Clean Up Your Facebook Profile 94

You Have One Shot to Pitch and Close a Deal 95

- Already Established Investors 96
- Creating Your Business Plan 99
    - Basic Business Plan Outline 101
        - Executive Summary 101
        - Company Description 102
        - Market Analysis 102
        - Organization and Management 102
        - Service or Product 102
        - Marking and Sales 102
        - Funding Request and Financial Projections 103
        - Appendix 103
    - Additional Tips 104
        - Research Everything You Can! 104
        - Define the Purpose of Your Business Plan 105
        - Create a Company Profile 105
        - Document Everything Regarding Your Business 106
        - Be Ready with a Strategic Marketing Plan 107
- Marketing to The New Target Audience 109
    - Know Your Customer Base 111
    - Figuring Out Your Target Audience 114
        - Gather Data from Your Current Customers 115

- Customer Data You Need to Know 116
- Use Website and Social Media Analytics Tools 117
- Facebook Specifics 118
  - Set a Goal 119
  - Target Your Ideal Audience 120
  - Use Images that Pop and Catch the Eye 123
  - Know What to Say and How to Say It 126
- You've Run Your Ads, Now What? 129
- Keep Your Eye on the Competition 131
- Methods of Income for the Non-Salesman 133
- Branded Weed Products 135
- Investing 137
- Crypto Currencies 139
- Getting Involved in Other Jobs Within the Market 140
- Real Estate Opportunities 142
  - Outdoor Grow Operations 143
  - Growing Facilities 144
  - Space, Ventilation, and Air 145
  - Let There Be Light! 148
  - Investing in Solar Energy 149
  - Reuse and Recycle Water 150

Designing Your Own Greenhouse 151

Security and Compliance for Growing 152

Promoting Cannabis-based Products............................154

Funding and Financing in Cannabis Ventures...............157

Conclusion 159

Acknowledgments

First of all, I would like to thank you for purchasing and reading this book. I am delighted that you're so interested in this unique and diverse world of cannabis-based businesses.

Secondly, I would like to thank my publishing company for giving me a voice in writing this book. I appreciate their faith in me to discuss this topic adequately.

Lastly, I would like to thank my friend Frank Fretz. I can't begin to thank him for his invaluable advice and pointing me in the right direction with my research.

Frank, thanks for your advice and I'm so happy you never grew out of your "hippy" phase!

Introduction

Since you've started researching this topic, I bet you're wondering, "What is all the hype behind this new cannabis craze?"

The greatest era of fascination with Mary Jane and her influence was in the United States during the '60s and '70s. However, recent legislation, medical studies, and general pop culture influences have led to a newfound openness and relaxed perspective on the drug.

Starting a business whose main source of income is selling marijuana is a bold move, to say the least. With dispensaries, websites, and CBD products popping up all across the United States and the rest of the world, millions of people are welcoming the new industry with open arms and open minds. Selling weed is no longer a backdoor transaction with a shady guy in the McDonald's parking lot.

The inescapable fact is that business is still business, no matter how simple selling cannabis may seem. While there will always be a consumer interested in buying the product, general business practices will still come into play as you grow your own enterprise. This means that if you're looking to make a substantial income with selling or investing in marijuana, then there are still necessary and crucial measures that need to be taken in order to ensure your success.

A few years ago, I had a friend who started taking his personal interest in recreational drugs to the next level. Although it was a fairly new topic of discussion, there was so much information out there that he was able to start making a passive income by investing in a legal marijuana business.

The fact of the matter is that cannabis is the fastest growing industry in the United States, and possibly the world.

Now, almost three years later, I've been able to pay off all of my debt and completely change my life. Before I could get to this point, I had a lot to learn when it came to ingesting, consuming, growing, distributing, and marketing weed.

My friend's small, but nonetheless undeniable, success at that time made me realize that right now was the perfect time to start looking into this opportunity. I knew next to nothing about the product, let alone the laws and licenses to attain before going into business.

It took about a year and a half of trial and error before I started making a decent profit. Now, my income has more than doubled, and I haven't looked back since.

But, what good is all my knowledge if I can't share it with others who want to change their lives too?

I decided to put everything I know about Marijuana and starting your own business selling it into one cohesive guide. This book provides you with all you could possibly need- or want - to know about marijuana: smoking it, selling it, the history and commercialization of it - everything!

Now more than at any other point in history ever before, the conversation behind cannabis is more relaxed and at the forefront of American and European culture. Why not capitalize on it?

Globally, there has already been a significant impact in several capacities involving the legal use of marijuana. From state and federal laws to business and marketing strategies to raising awareness and even finding cures for medical disorders and diseases; in one way or another, legal cannabis is changing the world.

Mind-altering substances, in one form or another, have generated more income on an individual-level than any other industry. The difference now is that selling and using marijuana is legal for recreational and medical use in many states, and federal laws permitting national legal use are expected to come into play within the next few years.

Here's another inescapable fact: right now is the most crucial time to start thinking about how you can invest your income and future into this rapidly growing industry.

While there are hundreds of ways to get involved in the cannabis business, licenses to sell or grow marijuana are not all that easy to obtain. However, once you get your foot in the door, whether it's opening your own dispensary or investing in the farms that grow the plants, you can change your life through this revolutionary industry.

As a small business owner, I already know the ins and outs of entrepreneurship. The minute details of establishing an LLC and finding a storefront to house my shop were things that I figured out along the way.

If it weren't for books and courses that taught me how to start my own business, then I would have never found the success that I did. That's why I felt so compelled to create this guide for you.

Coming up with an idea to make money is easy. Finding a way to take your thoughts that are on paper and making them a reality is the key.

Just like with any other financial investment, you're worried about the risk.

I get it.

As someone who was raised in a strict religious household having never had a drink until I was of legal age, getting involved with drugs (whether it was legal or not) was something I would have never considered.

Before you let the naysayers sway your judgment, consider the benefits of marijuana and how it is shaping our future. Unlike alcohol, there is zero evidence that any person has ever died from marijuana use alone.

In fact, a 2016 study found that for people between the ages of 15 to 49 globally, alcohol was the number one risk factor for death. What's even scarier is that the same study found that over 12% of male deaths were caused by alcohol.

Marijuana is also less addictive than alcohol and tobacco and has been used for over 3,000 years. While others may have their doubts about the legality of cannabis, it is by far the most regularly cultured, trafficked, and used prohibited recreational drug on an international level. As of 2016, more than 60% of the American population believed that the drug should be legalized.

Starting a new business can be scary.

Owning one that is as taboo as marijuana can result in even more pushback from friends and family and leave you feeling even more discouraged.

This book will make your journey that much easier. Instead of throwing a ton of information at you, I will breakdown the process of starting your business step-by-step making it easier than you ever thought possible.

Listen to me, and you will never look back.

Ultimately, I've done the whole punching someone else's clock for fifteen years. Investing my time and money into this lucrative opportunity was by far the best thing I've ever done.

I'm looking to retire in the next 5 to 7 years, instead of 20. Now is the time to take action, or you will look back in a few years and be sorry that you didn't.

Congratulations, you've taken the first step by reading this book! You've decided that you're going to tackle this challenge head-on and start your own legal marijuana business.

Don't let that fire in your belly dwindle down to ashes - light it up and keep it blazing (pun intended).

But in all seriousness, what exactly do you know about smoking weed? You roll it up in a piece of paper, sit back, light the tip, inhale, and enjoy, right? Not, necessarily.

While the action of smoking a joint may seem simple, there is a scientific reason why most people want to smoke it. You've heard of baking it into a batch of brownies or using an oil of some kind to achieve a high.

But why can't you just eat, snort, or inject it like other drugs?

All of these are not only valid but logical questions. These questions are posed so that you understand starting your own marijuana business is going to be more than selling it hand over fist.

You want to actually get to know your product because a good businessman always knows exactly what he is selling and the purpose that it serves.

Cannabis has been used for over 3,000 years, and the industry is only gaining more interest. This serves as evidence that not only will marijuana be around much longer, but that it wasn't until recent decades that the plant was used for recreational use.

Turn the page, and let's begin. Your future is waiting!

Marijuana: A History

While it may come as a surprise to you, most indigenous civilizations did not grow cannabis to get high, but rather as an additional resource for herbal medicine.

For example, the drug was utilized as an anesthetic during surgery.

Experts surmise the earliest use of cannabis is was in 2737 B.C in Central Asia near areas that are now known as Mongolia and Siberia. The first unambiguous record of the plant being utilized for its psychoactive properties was in the written literature of the Chinese Emperor Shen Nung.

Nung's scripts detailed the powerful effect marijuana had on several medical ailments such as gout, rheumatism, malaria, and even forgetful and inattentive behavior. While the medicinal value of marijuana was the key component in the studies, there was still a mention of the mind-altering properties exhibited in the test subjects.

As you may have already guessed, ancient cultures also utilized cannabis as a tool for spiritual exploration and guidance.

Researchers have even found burned seeds in kurgan burial sites that date all the way back to 3,000 B.C.

Some of the tombs in the Xinjiang region of China and Siberia included large amounts of psychotropic cannabis, leading experts to investigate the caste system of that time on an entirely new level.

From China, the plant moved between coastal farmers who brought it back to Korea around 2000 B.C. From Korea, marijuana seed traveled through South Asia and eventually North Africa.

The drug became even more popular for recreational use in India, where it was hailed as an herb that relieved anxiety. While the religion of Islam banned alcohol consumption, marijuana use was welcomed and even encouraged.

Muslims introduced hashish into the regions of Persia and North Africa during the 12th century. It was also from the Middle East that the Scythians transported the plants to Southeast Russian from the Ukraine.

From Russia, the drug moved to Germany and then Britain in the 5th century during the Anglo-Saxon invasions. Marijuana seeds have also been found on the ships of Vikings. It is believed that the Vikings used pot to relieve pain during childbirth and to relieve toothaches.

While the most common purpose of marijuana in ancient cultures was to relieve ailments, the plant itself and its hemp fibers were used to make clothing, ship sails, food, and paper. However, the plants were not found in the Americas until the Spanish brought it over around 1545.

Because of its many uses, hemp became a commercial crop. It was cultivated in colonies in Virginia, Massachusetts, and

Connecticut, as well as at a Spanish settlement in the Southwest.

As popular as cannabis was during its original agriculture stage in the United States, political and racial influences contributed to the national criminalization verdict by the government in the 20th century.

By the time 1890 rolled around, hemp had been replaced by an even more lucrative crop in the south - cotton. While many medicines during that time contained cannabis, an even greater number of prescriptions had traces of cocaine or opium.

When the roaring '20s came about, marijuana sales skyrocketed, which may have been caused by prohibition laws. However, recreational use of the drug was, for the most part, limited to jazz musicians and others in the show business industry.

Jazz music became influenced by "reefer songs." Pot clubs sprouted up in every major city in the U.S.

Unlike what was observed as associated with the effects of alcohol, authorities believed that since patrons weren't making public disturbances while smoking that cannabis wasn't a social threat.

Marijuana was a part of the United States pharmaceutical industry from 1850 to 1942. It was typically prescribed for rheumatism, pain during childbirth, and nausea.

Until the 1930s, it wasn't uncommon for people to use the drug in public spaces. However, it was during that decade that the United States Federal Bureau of Narcotics began a smear campaign against the drug. They painted it as powerful, addicting, and a gateway for greater substance abuse.

Over the next thirty years, the reputation behind marijuana use slowly dwindled from the 50's "beat generation," to the 60's hippies and rebellious teenagers. Finally, the Controlled Substances Act of 1970 sealed the fate for pot use declaring it of having the highest abuse potential (along with LSD and heroin) and becoming illegal for medical use.

The eradication of the plant began in 1975 when the Mexican government sprayed their crops with herbicide paraquat. Before this occurred, Mexico has been the greatest importer for marijuana into the United States.

In more recent history, the zero-tolerance policies passed by the Reagan and Bush presidential administrations pressed for stronger and more restrictive laws with enforced prison sentences for possession and stricter border policies.

The "War on Drugs" brought about a significant cultural shift as well as impacted the reliance on imported goods as domestic agriculture soared. By the beginning of 1982, the Drug Enforcement Administration (DEA) began shutting down marijuana farms in the United States.

This motivated farmers to grow their pot indoors with controlled environments that allowed the plants to evolve so that they would grow in smaller sizes but produce larger quantities of bud.

Smoking marijuana, whether recreationally or medicinally, has only become taboo in the last 60 years. Prior to political intervention, drug use was not only a social norm, but also widely accepted in public spaces by the majority of races, ages, and genders.

The idea that marijuana is a harmful and bad substance that causes addiction and leads to additional drug abuse is a relatively recent construct. You can argue that laws prohibiting any form of pot are not only misinformed but outdated and inverted.

For the majority of its history, weed has been legal and utilized around the world.

The Science of Getting High

Indica

Morphology: Short and bushy; suitable for indoor gardens

Geographical Origins: Areas between 30 to 50 degrees latitude.

Effects: Tend to be sedating and relaxing with full-body effects

Symptom Relief: Anxiety, insomnia, pain, muscle spasms

Sativa

Morphology: Tall and thin; suitable for outdoor gardens

Geographical Origins: Areas between 0 and 30 degrees latitude

Effects: Tend to be uplifting and creative with cerebrally-focused effects

Symptom Relief: Depression, ADD, fatigue, mood disorders

Even though you may be interested in selling cannabis, you don't necessarily have to smoke it. However, every good salesman knows everything there is to know about his product.

You wouldn't buy a car from someone who couldn't tell you the make, model, gas mileage, and the engine type of the vehicle they were selling to you. Consumers want to buy from merchants they trust and can keep coming back to in the future.

Weed is more than just a plant that you light and inhale smoke from. There is a reason why you can get high from it, why some strains are more expensive than others, and why you have to break down the THC with heat.

Sativa vs. Indica

If you were to wander through a dispensary, you would notice that strains of pot are broken into two distinguishable groups or subspecies of the marijuana plant. These strains are *sativa* and *indica*.

While they basically originate from the same type of plant, they both have completely different psychoactive properties and effects which result in different highs.

Sativa is the most common form of marijuana, providing a more uplifting and energizing high that pairs well with social outings and mentally and physically demanding activities.

Cannabis sativa was named by Carl Linneaus during the 18th century to describe the properties of hemp plants discovered in Europe and West Asia in an era when it was most cultivated for its fiber and seeds.

The Indica strains are the ones that are most commonly showcased in pop culture. They are mentally and physically sedative with a very relaxing effect. Cannabis indica was identified by Jean-Baptiste Lamarck in his report of the plant's psychoactive strains found in India as it was farmed for fiber and hashish.

It is often the slow-thinking and non-cognitive characters in movies and television shows that perpetuate the stigma surrounding marijuana's effects based on the experiences of using indica strains.

While typical marketing and advertising campaigns heavily rely on the separation of these two strains, cannabis experts have suggested that there is little evidence to show that a strong chemical profile exists in either that would strictly promote invigorating or sedating side effects.

What this means is that since we are all unique, the way we consume marijuana as well as which strains we use will not always affect us in predictable patterns. The dissimilarity between strains is going to matter to you most because the buds look and grow differently.

Why Strains Matter

Whether you are looking into cultivating the plants either by yourself or with additional partners or simply selling cannabis, you should still be able to recognize the distinctions between the plants.

You may be wondering why all this information should matter to you when you're just looking to sell the stuff, not smoke it.

Knowing what makes your bud better than what other dispensaries are selling is what will set you apart from every other person looking to get into the industry.

Your customers are going to ask you about the strains you're selling, where you're getting them, and they will compare your prices and products to every other product out there.

Consumers want businessmen that are going to level with them in terms of quality and pricing. Getting high doesn't mean smoking yourself into a vegetative state.

There is a reason why consumers choose to use marijuana over other narcotics.

THC and CBD

The cannabis plant is made up of hundreds of compounds that create singular one-of-a-kind effects primarily sustained by cannabinoids and terpenes.

You may have heard of THC or CBD. These are the two most common cannabinoids that are the primary drivers of marijuana's remedial and restorative effects.

The scientific name for THC is tetrahydrocannabinol, and it can make the user feel high, hungry, and is a sedative to treat ailments like pain or nausea.

CBD, also known as cannabidiol, does not contribute to the "high effect," but will relieve pain, inflammation, stress, anxiety, and other medical symptoms and disorders.

Strains that are THC-dominant are bought by customers who are looking for powerful and blissful experiences.

THC is known to treat anxiety, insomnia, and even depression. However, high quantities of THC contribute to cottonmouth, dry and red eyes, the munchies, and paranoia during a high.

Not everyone is as accustomed or receptive to the effects of THC. It's a potent compound that can either make your high a great experience or a miserable one.

Strains that are CBD-dominant contain less THC so that you can still reap the benefits of marijuana while maintaining a level head. Balanced strains that are near- equal parts of THC and CBD promote the best of both worlds.

You can maintain a mild high while experiencing relief from medical ailments that inhibit you from enjoying everyday life. A balanced strain is a perfect introduction to the world of marijuana use for individuals who are curious but have never tried it.

What Happens When You "Get High"

For you to learn how and why THC gets you high, you need to have a basic understanding of how our bodies process the food and chemicals that we ingest.

From the moment you take a bite of food, your body attempts to breakdown the chemical structure and decide what to do with it according to what it needs to use versus what it needs to get rid of.

Pharmacologists identify this 4 step process as "ADME," an acronym meaning Absorption, Distribution, Metabolism, Elimination.

Absorption

Absorption occurs within minutes of smoking weed. This happens so quickly because it is when the THC enters the bloodstream at concentrated amounts of 10% to 30%.

Distribution

Distribution is when the THC is attracted to and accumulates within fatty tissue. This includes the major organs, even your brain. This is why avid smokers will tell you that THC and its metabolites can remain in your system for up to 30 days, making it detectable during a urine drug test.

Metabolism

Metabolism is when your body metabolizes THC. This process occurs primarily in your liver using hepatic enzymes to break down the chemical.

THC elicits these enzymes, which can be dangerous to individuals taking prescription medication because they also rely on those same enzymes.

Elimination

Elimination is the last step of the process. The estimated time it takes for the THC to leave the bloodstream varies from person to person. This timeframe can range from as little as 6 minutes to as long as 22 hours.

This is not to say that you can stay high for 20 hours. Pharmacodynamics characterizes the interaction between THC and CB1 (the brain's primary receptor) in how long THC will be bound to the receptor and which other parts of the brain will be affected.

What it Means to Feel "High"

So, what does all this science jargon mean? When I first learned about why we get high when we smoke, I was basically bored to tears.

As someone who had never "experimented" with drugs before, all I really cared about was what it feels like to get high.

Ultimately, I had to eventually take the plunge and see what the hype was all about.

What does it feel like to get high? Honestly, it depends on the person and a few other factors.

The type of product you choose to use as the method of consumption will drastically affect your reaction in completely different ways.

For example, oils, primarily in the form of edibles, consist mostly of THC and give you more of a body high that kicks in around 30 to 60 minutes after eating them. The high can start winding down about 4 to 6 hours later.

Smoking, however, gives you a combination of THC and CBD, creating more of a mental high that begins only a few minutes after smoking and lasts between 2 to 4 hours.

The way you consume cannabis will play a large part in what kind of high you'll get. Edibles are extremely powerful because of their concentrated THC levels. However, the setting of the space where you are getting high can also play a large role.

I'm sure you've heard of people getting paranoid when they're high.

Even the most chill person can become suspicious if their mental state is corrupted.

If you are in a safe place with people you trust who just want to have a good time, then the odds are that you'll have a pretty relaxed and fun high. However, the opposite is also true.

If you're smoking in your car, you may be afraid of getting pulled over by the police or feel anxious about driving home under the influence, resulting in paranoia.

This is all because your senses are heightened when you're high. Smells, tastes, and textures can either be really pleasant or unwelcome. This is also what can inspire "the munchies," when you consume large amounts of food in sometimes abnormal combinations (such as olives and chocolate).

All in all, setting the mood also means setting your mental state. Put on some music, sit back, and enjoy the experience in a safe and welcoming environment.

The Commercialization of Marijuana

We have all at one point heard or seen a reference about marijuana in pop culture. From movies and television shows to songs and music videos, cannabis has become a deeply rooted inspiration and muse in today's media.

Marijuana in Pop Culture

I bet you didn't know that almost half of the R&B and hip hop music in the United States references marijuana in their lyrics. In fact, a recent study found that there is more allusion to weed and other drugs in the music industry than ever before. But, how does this influence the decriminalization of cannabis and promote usage among listeners?

The Entertainment Industry

On a historical level, any characters who smoked weed in TV shows or movies were dramatized through the perpetuated "lazy stoner" stereotype. This archetype was used more like the butt of a joke than an actual asset to the storyline.

I remember watching *That 70's Show* where a group of friends in high school sat in a circle in the protagonist's basement sharing a joint and a few laughs. At the time, smoking weed felt like a foreign and dangerous concept that only the bad kids in school actually tried.

The normalization of cannabis is driven by these media influences. From Cheech and Chong guest starring in recent shows to Scooby Doo and Shaggy having the munchies while the rest of the gang pursued their ghostly adventures, the characters from these iconic shows now seem outdated and an outlier in the true modern nature of cannabis use.

A more recent example of what marijuana users look like lies in the television show *Weeds*. In this Showtime series, suburban mom Nancy turns to selling marijuana to other parents and kids in the neighborhood after the sudden death of her husband leaves her without an income.

The first episode literally shows her selling drugs at her child's soccer game. What shows like this do is open our minds to new users who, for you and me, become an entirely new pool of customers.

So, while you can expect that college kids and twenty-somethings will certainly bring in some business, 40-year-olds and baby boomers are a huge part of the market, too. This demographic also tends to have a more stable disposable income.

There is basically an entirely new genre of movies dedicated to stoners that have only become more widespread. The greatest comedy actors of today are shown holding bongs and hotboxing in tons of movies, making weed seem cool and totally normal.

People watch these movies and see that the characters don't think of smoking weed as a big deal and associate marijuana with the exhilaration of comedy.

Music

Turning back to how the music industry will influence your sales, maybe music videos of half-naked women twerking on a smoky dance floor while a famous rapper enjoys a blunt aren't the best selling points for your business. Unfortunately for aspiring business owners in the industry, this is the image that has been instilled in our brains for decades.

The mentality of 'if you smoke marijuana, then you're a bad person' has shaped the world's view of weed for decades. This ideal is a key factor in the pushback against the decriminalization movement.

Even artists who have vocalized their support of cannabis use have come under fire and were silenced for their advocacy attempts. Think of Bob Dylan's song "Rainy Day Woman #12 and 35," which was banned from radio stations in 1966 for the lyrics "everybody must get stoned."

R&B artists and rock bands have both contributed to the rising use of weed since the '70s and given more fuel for government agents to push for stricter prison sentences for people caught with the drug or paraphernalia.

Looking at references today, public acceptance of cannabis for recreational and medical use has grown substantially since the '70s, driven heavily by the mentioning of cannabis in the Top 40's music.

Believe it or not, tobacco was not even mentioned in any of the most popular songs within the last few years; changing the social acceptance of tobacco usage in America to become more stigmatized than marijuana use.

Social Media

But music and movies aren't the only promoters of drug use. Between memes, YouTube videos, and everyone posting pictures from parties they went to the other night, social media has become the newest and most common platform for consuming pro-weed propaganda.

Online clothing brands plaster their shirts with the marijuana leaf symbol. Memes feature a stick figure with bloodshot puffy eyes making unique observations about the universe. More than 7% of Snoop Dog's social media posts involve drugs or alcohol.

All of these examples and countless more show that social media is an ally in the marijuana revolution. In fact, the hashtag for marijuana indicates that more than thirteen million posts are coupled with the tag.

Understanding Pop Culture and Weed Usage

Weed is becoming more mainstream than ever before. There are several outlets and citations that can help you understand cannabis culture and use it as you build your brand and business.

In a later chapter, I'm going to tell you exactly how you can use these influences and platforms to market to consumers of all backgrounds. Then at the right time, you can take your business to the next level.

While we all know that weed is present in different streams of media, I honestly didn't realize the impact that it had on society's view of the drug until I started digging a little deeper in my research.

The biggest consumers of media are young adults and teenagers, who are glued to their phones and computers almost 27/4. Even though your goal isn't to sell weed to a bunch of kids, understanding how pop culture shapes their perspective will ultimately allow you to create advertisements that will boost sales and create a lasting stream of income once your business hits the market.

Marijuana is everywhere you look. It's simply unavoidable.

Whether you are personally a fan of weed or not, you can't deny that acceptance rates of it have skyrocketed over the last 5 years. In the past, there were strict bans on all marijuana possession and use.

In 2019, 30 states have laws that permit legal use, 9 of which allow consumers to have the drug for recreational purposes. This is a time in history that no one ever thought would happen.

Prior to this new revolution of practiced potheads and curious newbies, there was a general lack of knowledge about the plant and little to no awareness about the benefits of it.

As scientific evidence surmounts to enlighten our perspective of marijuana use, the positives are slowly but surely outweighing the negatives.

More people than ever are finally waking up to the many benefits of using cannabis, and they want in on the action in one way or another.

Marijuana is finally being seen in a new light as a natural medicine that doesn't really live up to the decades of negative stereotypes.

New Legislation and Your Business

Snoop Dog and Rihanna may have played a role in the social acceptance of smoking weed. Many don't see getting high as such a big deal anymore.

A person using marijuana isn't seen as the lazy stoner who dresses a certain way and spaces out in a dark room. Celebrities have helped prove that you can retain the status of being a classy and sophisticated individual yet still enjoy a blunt.

With the help of celebrity awareness, the stoner stigma is slowly dwindling to a greater normalization of smoking weed.

While public approval of cannabis grows across the United States, uncertainty and vagueness around marijuana laws have provided a great opportunity for online distributors.

The public's eye is currently on Washington D.C., as the District is working on reforming current legislature.

Washington D.C.'s recreational marijuana law was approved via voter ballot in 2014. It legalized the cultivation, possession, and gifting of specific amounts of cannabis. However, selling the plant is still illegal.

Initiative 7, also known as the Legalization of Possession of Minimal Amounts of Marijuana for Personal Use Act of 2014, still left some ambiguity around where individuals can obtain recreational marijuana. This is where the struggle between federal and local government comes into play.

Now, state and local governments have the ultimate say when it comes to laws and legality within their borders. This has set the standard for many other states where marijuana possession and selling is legal.

The federal government makes the laws for all of the United States, right? The concept already makes for murky waters, but imagine that kind of power struggle is in the nation's capital.

Local politicians and the Department of Health in Washington D.C. have fought hard for full legalization of marijuana, as well as proposed methods to regulate the sale of the plant.

Congress has since stepped in to keep the District from taking the next steps towards legalization, even to the point of impeding the District of Columbia's funding. To this day, there are still debates between lobbyists and lawmakers on whether the regulations should be lifted.

This is a debate that goes much deeper than marijuana sales and restrictions.

Anyone in the District who is interested in using marijuana can have it and use it, but if the selling of a bud is illegal, how can they get it in order to smoke it?

Websites and phone apps, like LeafedIn.org, feature maps that show users where cannabis distributors are. The number of downloads on LeafedIn has only continued to grow in the last couple of years.

Because of the role technology has played in the distribution of marijuana, we finally have data to shine a light on the marketplace. For example, one of the founders of LeafedIn, John Khainson, found that the app indicated that there had been a significant increase in cannabis consumption in females. This data leads to the logical assumption that the industry has, for the most part, been male-dominated up until recently.

Restrictions are also giving aspiring entrepreneurs new and innovative ways to start making a profit in this uncharted market. Rather than selling marijuana, they "gift" the drug to thank customers for their purchase of other items such as clothing or food.

Brands are suddenly garnering awareness through weed, influencing buds to become an even greater staple through art and fashion.

What can you say? You can't keep a toker down.

In the last few years, we've seen an increase of states establish marijuana laws both for and against the drug. As public opinion for supporting the use of weed continues to grow, more states and local governments are also jumping on the bandwagon defining the terms of use within their borders.

However, the federal government is still the Big Bad Wolf in this scenario. Although the subject was touched upon in the 2016 Presidential elections, there has been little to no action or talk behind marijuana legalization. It still remains a secondary issue in the face of immigration and budgeting.

Examining State Laws

There are 33 states that have passed some sort of law defining marijuana possession, use, and selling.

Currently, these states have the most expansive recreational marijuana laws:

- Michigan
- Alaska
- Nevada
- California
- Washington
- Colorado
- Oregon
- Maine

- Vermont

- Massachusetts

- District of Columbia

For example, in November 2018, Michigan voters approve a new law for adults 21 and over to buy and possess marijuana for personal use. In 2018, Vermont was the first state to legalize weed through the legislative process instead of using a voter-based method.

The laws aren't as relaxed as you would think. Vermont's restrictions allow possession of one ounce or less of weed by an individual of at least 21 years of age to be treated as a civil violation rather than a criminal offense.

From there, the laws become even more strict with fines and jail time when more than two ounces is found on a person. This just goes to show that marijuana laws are much more complex than they really need to be.

It's knowing how to legally work with these laws and station your business in a safe way that is going to make the difference between your marijuana enterprise succeeding and you just wasting your money. After all, if you're going to be investing your hard earned money into this industry, you don't want to add even more risk than there already is.

Most other states have limited laws for the use of medical cannabis under certain circumstances. Like in Louisiana and West Virginia, you can only use cannabis-infused goods like pills or oils. Other states only allow patients with specific medical illnesses to have marijuana in their possession.

Other types of legalization include decriminalization of possessing small amounts of the drug. Even as the momentum behind legalization continues to reach new heights, traditional ways of thinking have kept local governments from jumping on board that the marijuana train.

This is once again where the struggle between state and local governments comes into play. Even though a state may legalize marijuana possession or use, certain cities or towns have the right to ban the drug and enforce punishment for individuals found with it.

Such is the case in New Jersey. Lawmakers of this state generally accept the movement towards legalization, although an official law has not yet been passed.

The greatest driver behind decriminalization in New Jersey is the legal sale of cannabis has boosted tax revenue in other states, which doesn't make legalizing the plant seem like such a bad idea. However, as the state begins to pave the way for new laws, about 50 local governments have already passed laws banning cannabis sales and possession in their townships and counties.

I can go on a whole rant in multiple paragraphs about state laws vs. federal laws, and different counties with their laws. But we both know you don't want to read pages upon pages of paragraphs upon paragraphs.

Weed Laws Listed by State

Enjoy the following list that will break down the individual laws for you through a much simpler explanation that will be easier to read and understand.

Let me note that the kind of licensing and documentation for you weed business will depend on the location. This entails not just the location of your enterprise, but also the type of business you are going to be running.

For example, a person who is growing and marketing cannabis to retail businesses could have other necessary permits than another person who is running a dispensary.

Alaska

The laws in Alaska allow the use of medical and recreational weed, with a few restrictions. It's legal to grow your own bud and possess up to four ounces in your residence. However, it is still illegal to sell or consume the drug in a public setting.

Businesswise, all you need to do is apply for a Marijuana Establishment License (which you can do online), along with submitting supplemental application documents for growing facilities, manufacturing and testing facilities, storefronts, and handler permits.

While this may seem like a lot of paperwork, there aren't as many hoops to jump through compared to other state laws.

Arizona

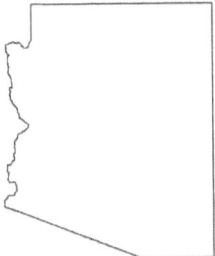

In 2010, just a little over 50% of voters passed the Arizona Medical Marijuana Act allowing possession and personal use of as much as 2.5 ounces of weed with written verification by a physician.

In Arizona, the medical marijuana program is actually run by the state Department of Health Services, which accepts dispensary registration certificate applications on a more inconsistent basis.

However, you can't set up a cultivation facility until you attain a license for a dispensary.

Arkansas

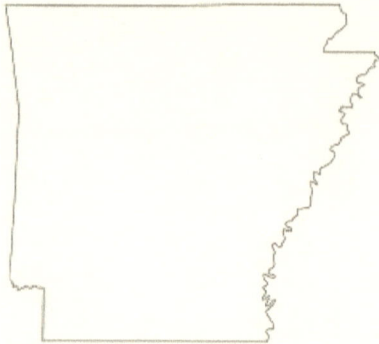

In 2016, Arkansas voters passed the medical marijuana law that allows the use of the drug for patients with cancer, PTSD, glaucoma, hepatitis c, and a few others diagnoses.

Unlike Arizona, Arkansas has its own department in the state government. The state's Medical Marijuana Commission is the primary authority for Arkansas's medical marijuana program. The Commission handles applications for dispensaries and growing facilities. The state's drug laws give the court more discretion when it comes to deciding the punishment for illegal possession. For small amounts, an individual can face up to one year of incarceration. There is also a mandatory minimum sentence for possession of more than 10 pounds of weed or the sale of more than 4 ounces at a time. If you possess more than 500 pounds, it is considered presumed intention to traffic the supply.

California

It's obviously no surprise that California has really lax laws when it comes to marijuana.

Persons of the age of 21 and over can possess up to 28.5 grams of weed or up to 8 grams of concentrated marijuana.

Anyone over the age of 18 found with more than 28.5 grams of weed can face imprisonment for up to 6 months or fined up to 500 dollars.

As for selling weed, as long as you have a state and local license, selling marijuana for both medical and recreational purposes is totally legal.

Colorado

Colorado was one of the first states to legalize marijuana for recreational use with certain limitations. This has become ultimately a situation where federal laws still trump over local ones.

First, all buyers must be at least 21 years old. If a person is found with one to two ounces of weed, it is counted as a petty offense and punishable by up to $100 in fines. Using the drug in public can result in greater charges of fines up to $100,000 depending on how much is found.

When it comes to unlicensed cultivation, if a grower is found with 6 plants or less, it counts as a misdemeanor that is punishable by as much as 18 months in jail and $5,000 in fines. The more plants you are found with, the harsher the penalties are. Licenses for medical and recreational weed are available, through the medical marijuana business license and the retail marijuana business license.

Connecticut

The Connecticut Department of Consumer Protection is in charge of the state's Medical Marijuana Program. It accepts applications and handles licenses for both cultivating facilities and dispensaries.

However, only about 4 to 10 licenses are given out at a time. Connecticut has decriminalized possession of small amounts of weed. The law states that individuals under the age of 21 may face a 60-day driver's license suspension. In 2012, Connecticut approved the sale of marijuana for medical use. Since the law was passed, growing facilities are now kept to the same standards as pharmaceutical factories. Patients must have one of the 11 listed debilitating illnesses in order to gain access to medical marijuana.

Delaware

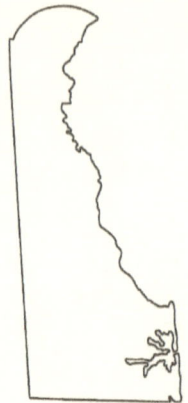

The Medical Marijuana Program in Delaware is a branch off of the Public Health Division. While medical marijuana is legal, there are still a limited number of distribution centers, which is probably because the state is one of the smallest in the country.

In 2015, the state introduced a bill to decriminalize marijuana entirely, which would mean that anyone caught with an ounce or less of weed would be given civil fines without a criminal record. As of 2019, persons found selling marijuana can face up to 5 years in prison and as much as $10,000 in fines. In the next year or so, you can anticipate drastic changes to these laws, as surrounding states take less dramatic offense to weed legalization.

Florida

Marijuana licenses and regulations are handled through a division of the Florida Department of Health, called the Office of Medical Marijuana Use.

The department is in charge of writing and enforcing the rules set by the department, as well as licensing businesses to dispense and cultivate medical cannabis.

In the Sunshine State, cannabis is illegal except in medicinal cases. Possession of small amounts is a crime. Possessing less than 20 grams on your person is a misdemeanor that can result in up to a year in jail.

Selling marijuana is considered a third-degree felony unless it is less than 20 grams.

Hawaii

Did you know that Hawaii has the tenth highest cannabis usage rate in the entire country? But, while Hawaiians have a reputation for smoking and growing quality weed, the plant is still illegal in the state. In fact, many tourists are slapped with fines and even jailed if found with marijuana. Imagine being fined for enjoying a joint while on vacation.

The Medical Cannabis Program is run by the Hawaii Department of Health. Patients with qualifying conditions are permitted medical marijuana use and possession of up to 3 ounces. With this permit, home cultivation is allowed for up to 7 plants at a time, as long as only 3 are mature.

The sale of any amount is considered a Class C felony. The more marijuana you're found selling, the harsher the punishment is. There have only been 8 licenses issued statewide.

Illinois

The Department of Financial and Professional Regulation is in charge of distributing licenses for dispensaries. The state Department of Agriculture is in charge of registering and regulating up to 22 growing centers.

Unfortunately, the application process for becoming a state-licensed cultivator is closed. Possession of fewer than 2.5 grams of weed is only treated as a Class C misdemeanor, resulting in a fine.

Selling up to 2.5 grams is considered a Class B misdemeanor.

However, medical marijuana is available for patients as of 2018, as long as they have a doctor's written recommendation and register with the state.

Louisiana

Louisiana used to have some of the strictest cannabis laws in the nation with hard labor convictions for certain instances. Fortunately, in 2017, Louisiana signed a law into legislation that set up the basis for patients and caregivers with written doctor's notice to obtain medical marijuana with protections through state-sponsored medical marijuana programs.

However, only a limited number of licensed pharmacies (approximately 10) have the authority to handle medicinal marijuana. While the law doesn't permit home cultivation of the plant, the penalties begin with misdemeanor status.

Possessing up to 14 grams can result in 15 days in jail and $300 in fines — amounts more than 14 grams will bring on additional jail time.

Maine

If you're looking to start a marijuana business in Maine, you'll have to go through the Division of Public Health Systems which is in charge of the Medical Use of Marijuana Program. Through the Division, you can obtain licenses for dispensaries although they are only issued one at a time.

Currently, there are about 10 dispensaries in the state. However, in 2018, aspiring entrepreneurs were able to apply for licenses to open retail marijuana storefronts and social clubs, which I imagine are similar to hookah bars.

Recreational weed is legal to the extent of each individual only possessing up to 2.5 ounces. It is also illegal to consume bud in public.

Maryland

In 2014, the state of Maryland passed a new law that decriminalized possession of smaller amounts of cannabis. The law is pretty generous in comparison to other state regulations.

In Maryland, an individual can possess up to 10 grams of weed at a time and only face a fine of $100 if found with it in public. The regulations and developing policies in Maryland are the responsibility of the Maryland Medical Cannabis Commission. It has already issued over 100 pre-approvals for dispensaries and companies, and an additional 20 have already been pushed through to the next step of the approval process. However, the unregulated sale of marijuana will result in fines and jail time. If a person is found selling under 50 pounds of weed, the felony charge would result in up to 5 years in prison and/or a $15,000 fine. As I'm sure you've already guessed, the greater amount you're found with, the harsher the sentence will be.

Massachusetts

In November 2016, the people spoke, and Massachusetts's marijuana law was changed.

The voters agreed to the legalization of recreational weed.

This means that adults over the age of 21 can possess up to one ounce of weed outside of their private residence and up to 10 ounces within their home.

Individuals over the age of 21 can also grow up to 6 plants at a time in their residences.

Maryland's Department of Health is in charge of the Medical Use of Marijuana Program, which deals with the applications for registered dispensaries.

Michigan

The Bureau of Medical Marijuana Regulation is in charge of overseeing the distribution of medical cannabis and is made up of two divisions: The Medical Marijuana Program and the Facility Licensing Division. In order to attain a license to open your own dispensary, cultivate, transport, and process weed, you need to go through the Department of Licensing and Regulatory Affairs.

Even though weed is on its way to becoming legalized for recreational purposes, residents can't buy it commercially right now. Cannabis sales are predicted to come into play early in 2020 as lawmakers iron out the details. However, after the certification of election results, persons over 21 years of age will be legally able to possess up to 2.5 ounces of weed in public and up to 10 ounces at home.

Minnesota

Minnesota proves that the Midwest is just as hip and up with the times as California. The state decriminalized cannabis possession to an extent. There is a $200 petty fine for possession of up to 42.5 grams. Although licenses to start a marijuana business are not available right now, the Department of Health of Minnesota has chosen two companies as the first registered manufacturers and distributors and has 8 dispensaries (or "cannabis patient centers").

In early 2019, lawmakers proposed a bill that would let the Department of Health regulate dispensaries and design a cultivation to sale system that would help local authorities regulate the production and sale of the plant in smaller communities. It would also prohibit advertisement towards adolescents, expungement of marijuana-related offenses from criminal records, and re-administer $10 million of the sales annually to help impoverished neighborhoods. That's a pretty rad deal.

Montana

Montana citizens have been fighting the good fight since 2004 when the state decriminalized medicinal weed for certain illnesses. In 2011, the legislature restricted medicinal use by limiting dispensaries to having only 3 customers each, as well as having the state evaluate doctors who prescribe bud to more than 25 patients a year.

Talk about a buzz kill.

In 2016, a vote was made to expand the number of medical conditions permitted to use marijuana as long as the patient has a state-issued registry identification card. Montana's Department of Public Health and Human Services is in charge of the Medical Marijuana Program in the state.

The department handles applications for providers, dispensary licenses, and testing laboratories.

Nevada

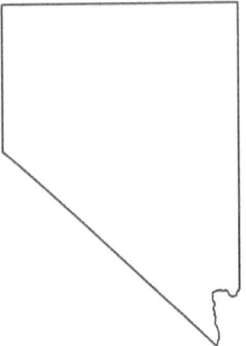

Viva Las Vegas and Viva Nevada's marijuana laws! In November 2016, Nevada locals voted to decriminalize weed.

As of January 2017, residents over the age of 21 can now buy, consume, grow, and possess up to one ounce of weed on their persons and even have up to 6 plants growing in their house at a time. The tax benefits are already influencing other states to lead towards legalization.

The Nevada Department of Taxation is in charge of licensing and regulating commercial cannabis businesses.

New Hampshire

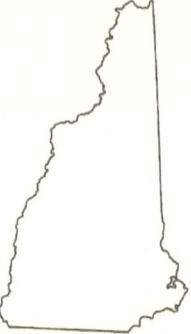

New Hampshire's policies are on the stricter side of the cannabis spectrum.

In 2013, the legislation was passed for medicinal weed, in which patients with a written doctor's recommendation could have up to 2 ounces of marijuana at a time.

The state law does not permit home cultivation, but there are 4 dispensaries in the tiny state called "Alternative Treatment Centers."

The New Hampshire Department of Health and Human Services is in charge of administering the state's cannabis program, but it unfortunately does not offer business license at this time.

New Jersey

The Medicinal Marijuana Program for New Jersey is run by the Department of Health.

Licenses for state-licensed marijuana businesses are called "Alternative Treatment Centers" and are granted permission to cultivate and sell medical marijuana.

So far, there are less than 10 dispensaries, and the state is not looking to issue additional permits for now.

Laws in New Jersey are looking to change in the next few years, especially as the subject comes to the forefront of the 2020 election.

New Mexico

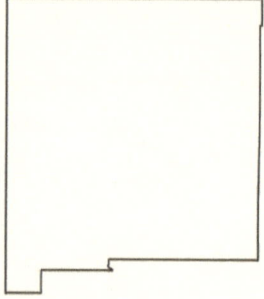

Although it's neighboring state of Colorado fully legalized weed, New Mexico is not necessarily on the same track. While the state legalized marijuana for medical use, possession is still illegal in other cases.

Penalties for selling cannabis depend on the seller's criminal background, location of the sale, and the amount of weed involved in the transaction.

If you're found in possession of one ounce or less of weed with medical documentation, it is considered a petty misdemeanor and can result in up to 15 days in jail and a fine between $50 to $100. The state's Department of Health is responsible for managing the Medical Cannabis Program.

To cultivate, transport, and sell medicinal weed, you need to apply for a Licensed Non-Profit Producer permit.

New York

New York has shown its blue colors in recent elections. While on many policies, it has leaned more towards the liberal side, its views on recreational weed are some of the strictest in the country.

There are dozens of different possession charges you can accumulate, and there has been little movement on the legalization front. New York allows limited use for medical marijuana and has restricted the number of dispensaries to only 20 in the entire state.

For those lucky 20, they can only sell non-smokable cannabis items such as edibles or oils. Possession of up to 25 grams will result in fines but no jail time. Any amount between 25 grams to 2 ounces can lead to as much as 3 months in jail and/or a $500 penalty. Selling or growing up to 24 grams of green can result in up to a year in jail and/or $1,000 in fines.

Only registered organizations through the Department of Health can manufacture and dispense medicinal weed.

North Dakota

North Dakota has relatively strict marijuana laws. Possession of even half an ounce is punishable by as much as 30 days in jail and a fine of $1,000.

If you're in possession of more than one ounce of weed, the charge is bumped up to a felony.

However, in November 2016, residents voted on Statutory Measure No.5 to legalize medical marijuana for the following conditions: AIDS, ALS, Cancer, Epilepsy, Glaucoma, and Hepatitis C.

The law allows residents to use medicinal weed if they have identification cards and certificates of registration. With eligibility, patients can have up to 3 ounces of weed at a time and even grow the plant in their house.

The Medical Marijuana Program falls under the responsibility of the Division of Medical Marijuana in North Dakota, which handles grower and dispensary applications.

Ohio

Ohio legalized medical marijuana in 2016, and the legislation came into full effect in 2018.

The Ohio Medical Marijuana Control Program administers permits for medical marijuana for patients with a written qualification from a physician and who register through the state's Patient and Caregiver Registry.

Dispensary application and registration can be done online through the state's government website.

Oregon

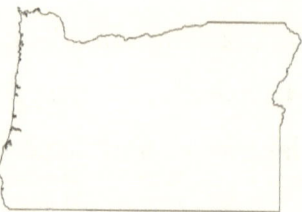

Oregon is one of the only states that has completely liberated its marijuana laws.

As of 2015, adults over the age of 21 can possess up to 8 ounces of marijuana for medical and recreational use.

You can also grow up to 4 plants in your residence at a time. However, recreational sales are restricted to medical marijuana dispensaries for now.

Oregon requires separate licenses for cultivators and dispensary owners, which can be attained through the Oregon Liquor Control Commission License.

Rhode Island

The Rhode Island Department of Business Regulation is in charge of overseeing and licensing dispensaries and cultivators in the state.

Applications can be presented during open application periods.

There are currently less than 5 dispensaries in operation.

Even though Rhode Island decriminalized marijuana and legalized access to the plant for medical conditions, possession of less than one ounce is a civil offense with a fine of $150.

The sale or cultivation of more than 11 pounds of weed can lead to a life sentence in prison.

Vermont

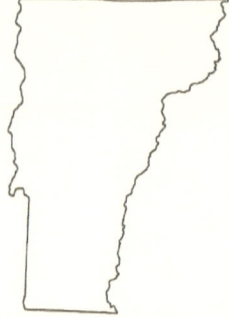

The Marijuana Registry is a branch of Vermont's Department of Public Safety.

The department has already issued four dispensary registration certificates and is looking to add more distributors to its list.

The state legalized cannabis in 2018 so that adults over the age of 21 can possess up to one ounce of weed at a time.

The law also allows residents to cultivate up to 2 mature plant sand 4 immature plants per residence.

Anyone under 21 years old will face fines and have their driver's license revoked.

Washington

Washington was one of the first states to legalize marijuana for recreational use. The plant is regulated by the Washington State Liquor Control Board which creates and manages regulations for zoning cultivation facilities and retail sales of weed as well as handle the applications for business licenses.

The law states that existing businesses cannot sell marijuana, but can sell cannabis-based products and paraphernalia. Consumers over the age of 21 can purchase and possess up to one ounce of weed. Businesses must have a license to cultivate, process, and sell cannabis.

Why Create New Laws?

If you were able to read through that whole list in one sitting, bless your heart. I hope it was a solid breakdown of state laws for you because even though marijuana may be decriminalized, that doesn't mean it's legal.

You don't want to be facing subpoenas and federal charges a month into your new business. Let's face it. There's more to cannabis businesses than just selling weed.

You have a ton of different options that are just as lucrative as opening a dispensary. But before I go into all of that, you need to know why these laws are changing and why legalization is becoming a primary issue in politics today.

From the "Just Say 'No'" campaign of the 1980s to Barack Obama taking a drag, times are changing, and we could see some sort of decriminalization or legalization laws coming into play in even more states in the upcoming 2020 presidential election.

Now, we know that federal laws ultimately trump any other legislation in individual states, but there is sanctuary within state lines to an extent. What this means is that even though you are technically safe under state law, you can still be prosecuted under federal law.

This is why the states that have legalized marijuana have such specific guidelines and medical qualifications. It's a tricky subject, to say the least.

State laws decide who can grow and sell weed, as well as determine the terms and conditions of the trade. The chart of the 33 states outlined above showed us a wide range of policies and regulations that come with these new laws.

By following state and local rules to perfection, you shouldn't have any serious problems when operating your business.

Why legalize weed in the first place? After all, we don't want teenagers abusing the herb and culture hasn't changed that much since it was made illegal, right?

Yes, both of those are weak arguments, but traditional values still believe them to be true and valid enough reasons to base national laws upon. When, in fact, there is more public support for cannabis law reform that at any other point in history. Recent polls are showing more than half the country is in favor of legalizing weed.

Reducing Harm

Reforming criminal marijuana laws will strengthen the effort of racial justice in the United States and begin the healing of communities most negatively impacted by the war on drugs.

Criminalization of cannabis use has disproportionately caused harm to young adults and people of color. It has also influenced greater levels of violence in low-income communities and has done little to dissuade youth interest and access to the drug.

As of early 2019, over 45% of incarcerations are for drug offenses. Approximately 200,000 people are in state prisons for drug-related crimes with another 82,000 inmates convicted in federal prison.

Convictions off of possession and petty drug "crimes," like selling, would provide more relief to the judicial system in all avenues and result in funding, therefore, creating more sustainable living conditions for inmates while giving more money back to the taxpayers.

The financial impact legalization will affect extends to other areas of the judicial system. Law enforcement resources that are already limited will be directed towards public safety. Both state and local governments would also gain additional tax revenue from legitimate cannabis sales.

Creating Jobs

The most efficient way to farm marijuana or hemp is to mass produce it. Someone is going to have to harvest the goods, right?

Marijuana is already one of the country's largest cash crops. Defining regulation laws will create jobs and profitable opportunities for the larger economy rather than the illegitimate market.

Reports estimate that by the year 2020, the legal marijuana market will produce more than a quarter of a million jobs. In 2016, the legal market was worth approximately seven billion dollars, and it's projected to continue growing at a compound annual rate of 17%.

You already know the positive impacts of the legalized marijuana industry, which is why you're reading this book. Aside from the agricultural impact, there will be dozens of other opportunities to make money through the cannabis industry.

Promote Consumer Safety

We've heard that drugs are bad our entire lives. While this may be the case for harder narcotics like heroin and meth, weed isn't actually a gateway drug, and the benefits far outweigh any negatives.

There is more information about the benefits of ingesting cannabis now than ever before. The internet has raised public awareness, and consumers are incredibly knowledgeable when it comes to safely using marijuana.

Cannabis product testing is becoming a requirement for the legal market. This means that consumers are not only better informed about the weed they use but are also getting their bud from reliable sources.

Medicinal Applications

The biggest push for legalization and regulation comes from patients and doctors who advocate for medical marijuana.

Why do patients find it helpful, and how can they talk about getting a prescription from their doctor? About 85% of Americans are on board with fully legalizing medicinal weed. At least several million patients are currently utilizing it.

Even though the majority of those who smoke weed are in it for the high, most medicinal cannabis products contain little to no THC. Cannabis has over a hundred active components, and CBD has little intoxicating effects. This means that patients who use medical marijuana only experience a little bit of a high that doesn't impact their cognitive function.

However, even without the glorious high of THC, patients consistently report the benefits weed has given them. From alleviating anxiety, curing insomnia, relieving turrets, to treating potentially fatal conditions, the evidence is mounting in favor of medical legalization.

One example of how great of an impact medical weed has is through the studies on Dravet syndrome. Severe Myoclonic Epilepsy of Infancy, or Dravet syndrome, is a form of childhood epilepsy that is nearly impossible to treat or control. However, it responds drastically to the strain of weed called "Charlotte's Web," which is CBD dominant.

The most common use for medicinal weed in America is for relieving pain. Although marijuana isn't strong enough to significantly impact severe pain, such as pain associated with a broken bone, it provides relief for chronic pain that millions of Americans suffer from.

It is impossible to overdose on and can take the place of pharmaceutical pain relievers like ibuprofen or aspirin. This is especially crucial for those with liver and kidney conditions.

Marijuana also appears to ease nerve pain, which is one area where few options for relief exist. Other effective medications such as Lyrica and Neurontin are incredibly sedative and affect a patient's ability to perform daily activities without feeling completely exhausted and disengaged.

In a similar manner, cannabis is also reported to be a great muscle relaxer which is life-changing for patients with Parkinson's disease, ALS, fibromyalgia, endometriosis, interstitial cysts, and most other conditions of chronic pain.

Weed is also used to treat:

- Weight Loss Management

- Post-Traumatic Stress Disorder

- Nausea

- Glaucoma

- Amyotrophic Lateral Sclerosis/Lou Gehrig's disease

- Autism

- Crohn's Disease

- Eating Disorders

- Cachexia/Wasting Syndrome

- Forms of Cancer
- Arthritis
- Dyskinetic Disorders (Disorders that are defined by involuntary movements)
- Spasticity Disorders
- Epilepsy
- Human Immunodeficiency Virus (HIV)/ Acquired Immunodeficiency Syndrome (AIDS)
- Huntington's Disease
- Insomnia
- Inflammatory Bowel Disease
- Irritable Bowel Syndrome
- Loss of Appetite
- Seizures
- Spinal Cord Disease

- Multiple Sclerosis

- Neurodegenerative Disorders (Conditions which affect the neurons in the brain)

- Peripheral Neuropathies

- Opioid Addiction and Dependence

- Parkinson's Disease

- Post- Traumatic Stress Disorder (PTSD)

- Severe Chronic Pain

- Sickle Cell Anemia

- Schizophrenia

- Terminal Illnesses and End of Life Care

My advice for patients who are seeking an open and honest conversation with their doctors about medical marijuana is to tell them that you consider this to be proper care and treatment and explain that you are educated about it. Your doctor should at least provide you with avenues for finding the right option for you.

Whether doctors are pro, against, or neutral about medicinal weed, patients are looking to it as a viable treatment option.

The fact of the matter is that patients will seek relief with marijuana one way or another. The safest option is for legal medical clearance nationwide.

Unfortunately, we are still gathering evidence to show just how useful cannabis can be in the medical field and how it can change the lives of millions across the globe.

Starting Your Legal Marijuana Business

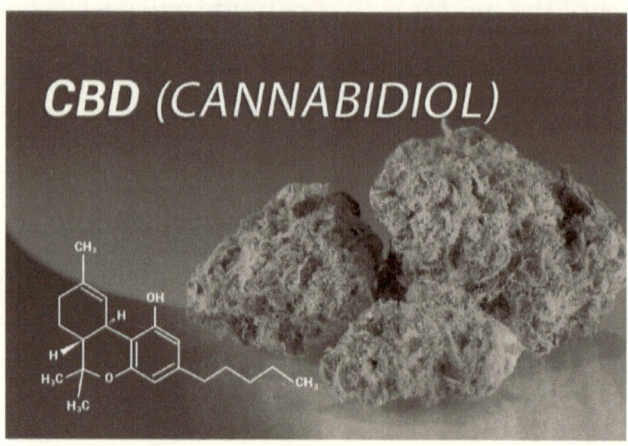

Finally! You're onto the part about making money now!

The rest of the book is going to go over everything you will need in order to launch a successful business in the cannabis industry. I think after reading the last two chapters, you understand what a tricky business selling weed can be.

You may feel a little discouraged right now if you live in a state that doesn't have any leeway for independently owned dispensaries. I was in the same position when I started.

I'm not from an ultra-liberal state where anyone can openly sell weed, and no one thinks anything of it. I'm a Pennsylvania resident all the way.

My heart lies in the farmlands. Pittsburgh and Philadelphia are the biggest cities I had ever visited before I started my business. The fact of the matter is you don't need to live in California to make a living, or even some side cash, when investing in the marijuana industry.

Regardless of where you live, this is a hot market that is only going to skyrocket as the government catches up to the inevitable change in culture. People like you and me are the ones paving the way towards the future.

Real Start-Up Costs

There are many economic factors that you must consider when you open a startup business. The budgetary factors that you must consider when starting a cannabis-related storefront include, but are in no way limited to:

- Rent or lease payments

- Employee payroll

- Utility bill payments

- State, city, and local license fees

- Merchandising and inventory purchasing

- Legal counsel and retention

- Liability insurance

- Zoning law restrictions

- Vendors to buy from

- Music license (if you plan to play copyrighted music on public speakers in a place of business)

Do you have the economic means to pay monthly rent or lease payments for a place of business? It's a serious matter not to be taken lightly.

The monthly rent for a storefront can cost you anywhere from several thousand to tens of thousands of dollars a month. Depending on your renting or lease agreement, such payments could be prone to unannounced increases as well.

Here is a chart to breakdown some common startup expenses:

Startup Expenses

Furniture	$15,500.00
Décor	$12,700.00
Designing	$7,500.00
Construction & Layout	$22,500.00
Menu and POS	$8,000.00
Equipment	$23,000.00
Rent and Insurance	$4,500.00
Legal and Licenses	$2,500.00
Stationery and Uniform	$1,800.00
Startup Cash	$5,000.00
Startup Inventory	$5,000.00
Total Startup Expenses	**$108,000.00**

These decisions require the help of financial and accounting experts. If you are not an expert, you need help. What is not covered in the above chart are ongoing costs like utilities, garbage pickup, and other regular monthly costs like phone lines.

Accommodations for these should be in your build out, and, of course, are necessary to open for business. Ongoing costs in your overhead will be part of your yearly operating costs and included in your business plan, which we will discuss in detail later.

Find a Niche That Fits a Need

I'm going to go through this one step at a time. I know you may not be the person who is interested in owning a dispensary or just investing in the operations of a manufacturer, but the business is the business.

As one of the oldest careers in human history, growing and selling drugs is almost everyone's go-to when they want to break into the industry.

So, you want to start your own marijuana business? Well, the first thing you've got to do is have a unique idea that fits an unfulfilled need in the industry.

Just like with any industry, whether it's food or hospitality, you've got to have an "x-factor" that sets you apart from everybody else that you'll be in competition with. This is what we call a niche. Think of it like those 1950's themed diners where the waitresses wear pink aprons and roller skate, and the cooks talk in diner slang to make the experience feel like you've time traveled back to a simpler time.

There are thousands, if not millions, of diners out there. But it is a true experience to sit down and feel like you're back in the ages of poodle skirts and The Beatles when you walk into those themed restaurants. *This* is what we're going for with your cannabis enterprise.

Before you go investing your life savings into a new venture, you have to decide which sector of the cannabis industry to go into.

When someone thinks about different weed businesses they can invest in, dispensaries or manufacturing typically come to mind.

You're probably thinking of those huge dispensaries in California and Colorado raking in the dough when in reality selling weed can be the riskiest path to choose.

As marijuana gains legality across the United States, the price of weed will naturally go down.

This means that dispensaries and growing operations will ultimately suffer. In fact, those storefronts and manufacturers will be hit hardest by the new laws and regulations that will come into play later down the road.

To possibly burst your bubble even more, banks are still refusing to work with any businesses that are associated with growing and selling cannabis because weed is still illegal under federal law.

Now, don't be discouraged by this. Circumstances will change eventually, but you can't and don't want to wait until the laws change to start making money. This means that you will need to fundraise enough capital without using a bank as a resource.

How much will those initial startup funds need to be? Well, many states require evidence of at least one million dollars in immediate cash to gain a dispensary license.

It's also a good idea to keep in mind that you won't be able to store your profits in a bank account safely. Unfortunately, all enterprises that directly deal with marijuana are basically forced to keep their capital in cash, which can obviously be dangerous and pretty inconvenient. Fortunately, cryptocurrencies have given us a solution to this issue and added even more security to our funds.

The marijuana industry offers so much more opportunity than stores and dispensaries.

If you love trying new foods and creating recipes, then making your own edibles line could be a cool niche to get into.

There are even businesses called "bud and breakfasts" that are marijuana-friendly hotels. The Controlled Substances Act established federal drug policy in the United States in which the manufacturing, importing, possession, use, and distribution of drugs are strictly regulated.

This means that the regulations put in place by this law are only applicable to marijuana growers, processors, and distributors leaving a wide open opportunity for anyone who isn't directly in business with the plant itself.

This is why businesses that provide support to the primary organizations in the marijuana industry are doing so well. They get to avoid high taxes and political limitations.

From cultivation products and media companies to consulting agencies and professional training and education, the abundance of new technologies makes the opportunities endless.

If you're a tech-savvy inventor, you could design a product that allows consumers to ingest their product in a different way.

Think about all the new vape pens that have come out in the last couple of years or diffusers that dispense cannabis oil fumes.

I'm someone who believes that if you have a passion for something, then you can make it into a career or at least an avenue for side income. For me, my passion was business and marketing.

I'll give you an example from when I first got into the industry. I come from a corporate background so, I'm all about the bottom line and delivering efficient and effective products and systems for quality results.

Luckily for me, I lived pretty close to a college town and had the opportunity of cashing in on a key demographic of the marijuana consumer base of college kids. Even though most 20-something's in college don't have a steady stream of income, they are looking for convenience, and a means to bridge their inherent procrastination and their desire for weed.

That's where I came in. I provided safe and reasonably priced edibles, delivered straight to your door. This is what I mean when I say you need a unique creative idea that fills a gap in the industry.

When starting a business in the marijuana industry, aspiring entrepreneurs must first make sure that their idea is legally viable and offers a unique solution for the marketplace.

Too often, an idea is exciting but can't be supported within the legal limits, or it is just a recycled concept that is dependent on the first mover advantage in their area. In order to guarantee long term and scalable success, a company needs to be able to withstand progressive regulations and business factors in an ever-changing space.

Sounds a little overwhelming, doesn't it? No worries! You don't have to be an innovative genius or an ultra-creative person to make money in this industry. After all, it's usually the simplest and most efficient ideas that make the greatest impact in the business world.

To get your creative juices flowing, here are a few ideas to help you brainstorm your niche in the marijuana market:

Organic Beauty Products	Accessories
Delivery Service	Packaging
Marketing and Consulting	Product Reviewer

Cannabis Florist	Seed Distributor
Cannabis-Based Restaurant	Smoke and Paint Classes *think Paint and Sip, but with weed instead of wine*

Know What the Rules Are

Remember, as a kid, when you broke the rules when playing a game, and the teacher would put you in a "timeout?"

In this case, if you break the rules when running or starting up your marijuana business, you will have a "timeout" in jail.

Obviously, you want to avoid violating any regulations and laws. Any misstep can lead to huge fines and jail time.

Even if you have a genius business plan, enough funding, and customers ready to go, if you don't play by the rules, then you're going to get shut down faster than it took you to get started.

The laws and regulations for starting a marijuana business are confusing and complicated. I highly recommend that you hire an attorney experienced in cannabis law to help you navigate your way through this process to make sure that your new business is legitimate.

As a newcomer to the industry, I knew that if I was going to invest most of my life's savings into becoming an entrepreneur, I needed to get it right. There's already enough risk going into a business that involves weed, and I wasn't going to take my chances in the possibility of overlooking a regulation.

I did plenty of research to make sure that I got help from one of the most experienced marijuana attorneys out there. I reached out to other established business owners to get as much advice as possible.

You're already going to get enough input and criticism from everyone in your network but smoking a joint once in a while doesn't make you an expert. Make sure that you get the help from someone who has a clean background and checks out as a legitimate source.

As I've already explained, each state has different laws, and they are constantly changing. You can find even more detailed guides to cannabis laws online and do the research necessary to get started in your state.

Regardless of which state you're looking to launch your startup in, both medical and recreational cannabis businesses require a license for operation. To obtain the license, you will need to adhere to the state's laws and follow the application process to secure your legal status.

The top performers in most industries tend to look out for each other. Don't be afraid to contact the other dispensaries or investors in your local area for guidance.

The world is changing towards embracing cannabis use, so if just a few dispensaries or manufacturers are put into the hot seat by the media, it could put the entire industry in a negative light for the next two decades. You can also learn a lot from other cannabis business owners when it comes to branding, labeling products, and selling techniques.

Raising Enough Capital

With any new business, investment capital is essential to launching your business plan. Many investors aren't looking to put their money into marijuana businesses because it is still illegal under federal law.

You also have to look for banks who are willing to host your account and support your business. For now, focus on finding trustworthy and legit private investors who are excited about the fast-rising cannabis industry and the opportunities that come with growing markets.

Your investors don't have to be already involved in the cannabis industry, or even smoke weed to understand how to succeed with a startup.

Search for investors who can bring experience and knowledge from other industries because they have skill sets that will almost definitely come in handy at some point during the first few years of operation.

Marijuana partnerships are an obvious and smart method of extending your company. You have to find the balance between your excitement of having extra assistance and finding the right partners to work with.

You should also live by my number one rule of "never trust anybody but yourself." This means that you would always have a backup plan.

I went through several phases of finding the people that I wanted to go into business with. I had a couple of flaky people fall through, and others who I should have known were all talk and no game.

Finally, as the contracts were being drawn for an incredible relationship between me and my number one prospect, the guy changed the terms to take advantage of the situation.

Hence, my advice of never trusting anyone but yourself and to always have an exit strategy. Sometimes, it takes going through some harder experiences to teach you how to play the game efficiently.

Clean Up Your Facebook Profile

Okay, not just Facebook but every social media profile you have needs to be squeaky clean. You would be shocked by how many deals are made through social media.

These platforms are easy to work your network contacts and make connections with people who can not only invest in your business but also take it to the next level.

This means that you need to carefully craft your profiles so that they are appealing to prospective investors and promote an image that says you're serious about your business. At the end of the day, investors and companies are investing in people, not just their ideas.

You Have One Shot to Pitch and Close a Deal

It may sound dramatic, but it's true nonetheless. You have one chance to pitch your business idea and close that deal.

You have to have absolutely every detail accounted for. Simply having an idea and name isn't enough to sell someone on your business.

If you're looking for funding, you need to be prepared with facts, figures, projected sales, and undeniable knowledge of the market and industry. This is true with any business, not just the ones that involve marijuana.

Have you ever watched the television show *Shark Tank*? It airs in countries around the world featuring some of the most prominent, affluent people who are self-made millionaires being pitched ideas and businesses from people wanting to become successful entrepreneurs.

After the flashy presentations, what the sharks really want to hear are the cold, hard facts.

> ➢ Is there really a market for that product?

> ➢ How many units have you sold?

- What is your revenue so far for this year, the last two years?

They want to invest in someone they can trust with their money. Take all of these factors into consideration as you prepare your pitch.

Already Established Investors

This next part of the process will hopefully help you catch somewhat of a break. You're the new kid on the block, and you're probably starting to feel overwhelmed by all of this information coming at you. Don't get discouraged and stay motivated. No one said that being your own boss or starting a side business would be easy.

To help ease your worries and make this process a little bit easier, I've included a few investment firms and businesses who are actively looking for startups in the cannabis industry.

- **Altitude Investment Management** – A United States based global venture capital fund that invests in a wide range of companies that are in their early stages.

- **Cannabis Capital LLC** – Looking for an investor to help jumpstart your business? Cannabis Capital

LLC is an investment firm with the mission to connect revolutionary ideas with investors with capital.

- **Ganjapreneur.com** – Ganjapreneur may appear just to be a resource for aspiring weed professionals, but it is also an invaluable tool to help you connect with other business owners, investors, and vital recent news in the legality of marijuana on a global basis.

- **Green Acre Capital** – A private investment fund that assists newcomers in the Canadian medicinal and personal use weed industries.

- **Halley Venture Partners** – This venture capitalist firm only invests in the legal marijuana industry. These partners are here for you every step of the way, along with supplying the funding you need to take your business to the next level.

- **Merida Capital Partners** – A private equity investment firm, whose mission is to assist fundamental growth drivers through support in the development of the cannabis market.

- **Navy Capital** – An investment company located in New York City, seeking to find the best in new business venture within the cannabis industry.

- **Tuatara** – Tuatara invests in established industry leaders in their legal cannabis ventures.

Creating Your Business Plan

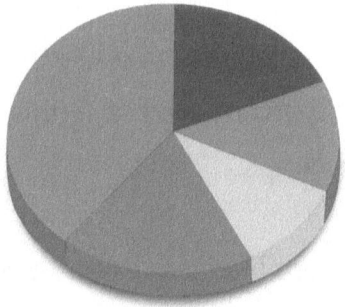

The saying goes that you should save the best for last. In this case, I reserved the most important piece of information for last because it requires the most of your focus and the utmost attention to detail.

Your business plan is the most crucial aspect of starting your own weed-related business.

Fortunately, there are dozens of different products, services, and industries that fall under the marijuana umbrella.

Are you interested in the science behind creating the perfect strain? Are you interested in the lifestyle of normalizing weed in modern society? Do you like clothing or have a green thumb?

Maybe your thing is the craftiness of consumption through various apparatuses and paraphernalia.

You have an endless amount of opportunities and finding the right soil to fertilize your seed of genius is what will skyrocket you to success.

Anyone who has zero business experience may be wondering, "what is a business plan?" It is basically a single document detailing everything that you envision your business being.

It's more than just a one-page summary. It goes into detail about your mission, marketing strategy, competition, market analysis, and development plan.

You may be one of the lucky ones who don't necessarily need outside funding, but that doesn't mean you should skip this vital step.

A business plan outlines your goals to see where your pitfalls and blind spots are so that you can get ahead of any mistakes.

Basic Business Plan Outline

A business plan is two things:

- ➢ A roadmap to the success of your restaurant focused on reaching your financial and personal goals.

- ➢ A road map to obtaining financing, persuading others to invest in your dream.

Writing a business plan sounds like a daunting task, but it shouldn't be. Just be clear and concise. Keep it short. No one is going to read hundreds of pages that you have slaved over. Start with a cover page followed by a Table of Contents then go on from there.

You should also plan on revising and changing your business plan as your business evolves. This is a living, breathing document and is not set in stone.

Executive Summary

This first introductory part is a small snapshot of your idea and how it will work in the real world.

Company Description

What does your business do? What needs does it fill in the market, and what is your mission statement?

Market Analysis

A cohesive breakdown of data of your market research. You want to include information about the industry, consumers, and competition.

Organization and Management

How will your business run? Will you be supervising production, leading as a key investor, or picking the bud yourself?

Service or Product

This is your opportunity to go in depth about what you're offering to consumers. What makes your product different? What will your services bring to this niche industry?

Marking and Sales

Outline your marketing and sales strategies. Are you going to use social media or hire an outside advertising agency?

What prices do you need to market your services for in order to break even or make a profit?

Funding Request and Financial Projections

Now is the time to use all the great data you've gathered to your advantage.

Breakdown how much money you'll need for the next three to five years of operation.

When outlining these projections, realistically consider how your business will grow and change in the next few years.

- ➢ Are you going to hire more employees?

- ➢ Are you looking to move into a bigger warehouse?

- ➢ Where do you want your business to go, and how much money will get you there?

Appendix

Provide a section that acts as a guide to the entirety of the document, as well as your resume and permits for operation.

Additional Tips

A well thought out business plan can be your best ally in the future assisting you with making good business decisions especially when it comes to deciding the how's, when's and where's of allocating your resources.

A business plan also provides specific and organized information about your company and how you will repay borrowed money.

Research Everything You Can!

Research, research, research!

Analyze and research absolutely everything you can about your product, the market, and deepen your expertise on the industry. You should spend at least twice as much time researching and evaluating as you actually spend writing your business plan.

To create the perfect plan for your company, there isn't a single fact or factor you shouldn't already know.

As the owner and visionary, it is your responsibility to know everything about the industry you are entering.

Define the Purpose of Your Business Plan

Entrepreneur Magazine defines a business plan as "a written document describing the nature of the business, the sales and marketing strategy, the financial background, and containing a projected profit and loss statement."

While one useful reason to create a business plan is pulling in investors, it can serve several purposes.

A business plan is a road map that gives you direction, so you can plan ahead for the future and avoid any bumps in the road.

Create a Company Profile

When you are just launching a new business and are itching to make a great first impression on prospective consumers, then it is essential to craft a company profile that makes an impact.

A profile that is well-written and driven by passion is an effective way to present your company to other stakeholders and customers.

Your company profile should include:

- The history of your business

- The main product or services that you'll provide

- Your target audience and market demographics

- Where your supplies will come from

- What problems your company will solve

- What makes your idea unique

Document Everything Regarding Your Business

When looking for investors, you need to have evidence ready to show that you can make them money. This means that everything you know about your business your investors want to know, too.

Remember when I said that investors are not just investing in an idea, but the people behind it?

You have to prove yourself and your company through hard documentation of your expenses and cash flow, industry projects, and even minor details like your storefront strategy, permits, and licensing agreements.

Be Ready with a Strategic Marketing Plan

Just because you're a newbie doesn't mean that you shouldn't be playing hardball. As a new business owner, you have to be aggressive with a strategic marketing plan.

Include the following marketing objectives in your outline:

- New Products

- Long-Term Contracts with Clients

- New Geographical Territories

- Extending the Market for Existing Products

- Creating Efficient Manufacturing and Delivery Methods

- Boosting Sales for a Specific Product

- How to Raise Prices without Cutting Sales Figures

- Cross-Selling Products

- A Content Marketing Strategy

Your marketing objectives should include several smaller goals outlined to help you attain your larger objectives. You want to focus on the 'what' and 'why' of your marketing initiatives for at least one year ahead.

You want to include the practical implementation of your strategies addressing the who, why, when, where, and how.

What percentage of your budget will go towards marketing? What are your sales goals for the next few years?

These are the questions you need to answer before showing your business plan to investors.

Marketing to The New Target Audience

It seems like everyone has a base knowledge of marketing nowadays. We're in a unique age where a huge portion of the population is connected to a device that allows businesses to reach their customers directly.

Cell phones, tablets, and any other technology with access to the internet is dominated by ads and campaigns. While traditional methods of advertising like radio and television commercials may still reach consumers, websites and apps are cheaper to use as platforms to reach consumers and will generate sales on a much greater scale.

The thing is that you don't have to be a tech wiz or advertising genius to make a significant income with sales or to drive customers through your door.

In this chapter, I'm going to break down simple but effective ways to market your business. Even when taking marijuana out of the equation, the marketing principles are the same no matter what industry you're in or what products you are selling.

It also doesn't matter if you're looking into growing and selling bud or creating products that allow customers to consume cannabis, advertisements will allow your business to skyrocket if done correctly.

To be honest, there are literally hundreds of articles that will teach you how to publish an ad, create a branding graphic, and literally walk you through SEO techniques.

Once you push past the barrier of resistance and laziness, you become an unstoppable force in the business world.

You're reading this book because you want the best information handed to you without any strings attached. You're doing what 99% of the population won't, which is taking action.

In this sense, you're already winning.

This chapter will take the information that I've found to be the most efficient, and break it down for you to understand and implement in your own business.

Know Your Customer Base

Now that you have a winning idea for your business, the most important information is *who* is going to be interested in your service or market.

You may already have some foundational knowledge or familiarity when it comes to consumer research. As a business owner, you want to know exactly who your customer is from their age and height, to how they drink their coffee and spend their Saturday nights.

You want to understand your customer's wants and needs on a deeper level to know exactly what they are willing to invest their money in and how it helps them.

Think about the way children's movies are made and marketed. In addition to the psychedelic cartoons and colors, the general storyline features relatable characters that teach an overall heartwarming life lesson that leaves the viewers feeling warm and fuzzy in the end. But, there's also some adult humor for those over the age of twelve because the director and scriptwriters know that parents will be taking their little ones to the theaters.

What else do we know about children's movies? They usually premier on days that kids have off from school like Christmas Day or Easter Weekend. They don't show kids movies after about eight o'clock at night because parents most likely won't be taking their kids to the theater that late.

The characters are identifiable, often younger with big adventures ahead where they can be challenged and make new friends, much like the children who are watching the film.

All of these seemingly small observations are actually the foundation of the success of every blockbuster.

When you come up with an idea for your marijuana business, you need to conduct comprehensive and accurate cannabis-focused market research to understand who will be buying your products or services and how it will serve their lives.

The cannabis industry is unique with its own challenges that don't have concrete solutions.

With these unanswered questions and foundation for unfiltered creativity, it's your job to understand your consumer base and the unfulfilled need you are meeting for them.

Because the marijuana industry is so new, it is unlike any other market out there.

The regulations, supply chains, banking and taxation, marketing, and stigmas surrounding the business can take away from your profits and distract you from the essential features of your business.

One of the greatest challenges you'll face is the overcrowding of the space, which is why understanding who your core consumers are and what products they want the most is key in targeted consumer segmentation.

Figuring Out Your Target Audience

Defining your target audience is one of an entrepreneur's most crucial tasks. It is the foundation of all components of your marketing strategy, from how your products are created and named to the marketing channels you utilize to promote them.

One of the greatest mistakes new business owners make in branding is trying to appeal to everyone. A target market or target audience is the specific group of people that you want to reach with your ad messaging. They are the ones who share common characteristics and are the most likely to buy your products.

The more clearly you're able to define your target audience, the better you can develop your marketing strategies as well as how and where you can reach that demographic.

First, start with a broad category. An easy one is millennials which comprise of any young adult born between 1981 and 1996.

Already, you've limited your range. Now, it's time to get highly specific to attain the best possible conversion rates. It's all about targeting your advertising efforts effectively to encourage a steady flow of customers.

The people who don't fall within your target audience can still buy from you. They're just not the focus when it comes to creating your marketing strategy.

Gather Data from Your Current Customers

Identify who is already using your products and services to figure out the people who most want to purchase from you.

Once you understand the characteristics that define your present customer base, you can target more people who fit into the same demographic.

If you're like me, you may be starting this new business without any sample size to use as a starting point for your marketing tactics.

I had to do a lot of my own research and go off of what I knew college kids wanted in general, then readjust my perspective to fit what I knew about the marijuana industry.

Gather any information you have about your existing consumers into a database, and you can track trends and anticipate their needs before *they* even realize what they are.

Customer Data You Need to Know

- **Age**. You do not need to know how old each person is that buys from you. It won't really make a difference if your average customer is 25 or 28. But, identifying which decade of life or generation your customer is in can prove to be useful information.

- **Location**. In terms of time zone and geographical area, where do your current customers live? Along with understanding which geographic areas to target with your marketing, knowing your customers' location can help you figure out what hours of operation best fit your customers' needs in terms of sales, service, online assistance, and when you should launch ads and posts on social media.

- **Language**. Even though you may fit your own target audience, you can't assume that your customers will speak the same language as you. In addition, don't make the assumption that your target market speaks the dominant language of their current geographic location.

- **Spending Capability and Patterns**. How much money do your customers have to spend on your products and services? How do they approach purchases for products in the prices you offer? Do your customers have financial limitations or concerns that you can address through your services?

> **Interests/ Hobbies.** Obviously, your customers like to get high. But what do they like to watch on TV? What other businesses do they buy from? What do they do with their valuable free time? Time is the most valuable thing you have, so how are your customers spending their time?

> **Stage of Life**. Are the majority of your customer in college? Are they parents or retirees? A person's stage of life can say a lot about their finances and how much they value quality in the products they buy. For example, a college kid will spend his last ten dollars on a cheap bottle of tequila, while a middle-aged woman knows the luxury in a quality whiskey.

Use Website and Social Media Analytics Tools

As someone who hasn't even started their new business, you're probably wondering how to get this kind of information efficiently. This is where social media analytics can fill in the gaps in your consumer analysis.

They can also clarify for you who is actively interacting with your social media accounts, even if they haven't bought any of your products yet. Any simple Google search can help you find complete guides on how to use analytics on every major social network.

Facebook, Pinterest, LinkedIn, YouTube, Twitter, and Instagram are all platforms that can help you make more money and reach a greater customer base. These guides will help you gather priceless data that helps define your customer characteristics, find out what other interests your consumers have, and how you can integrate them into your marketing to contribute to your overall success in the marijuana industry.

Facebook Specifics

I'm going to break down Facebook analytics for you, just so you have a basic understanding of how advertisements work on one of the world's largest social media platforms.

Facebook ads are one of the cheapest and easily trackable methods of internet marketing. They also give you more control over your advertisements, so you're less likely to waste your money. The following are ten of the most efficient tips for running successful advertisements on Facebook ads.

Set a Goal

You're running an ad to make money, that's obvious. But who are you trying to reach? How many clicks or views are you trying to get? What are you hoping your conversion ratio will be? To run successful ads on Facebook, you need to answer the question of "what do you want your ads to do?"

Aside from earning more income, think about how many sales or followers you want to obtain. Do you want more engagement from your customers and prospects?

Regardless of your general goal, Facebook marketing is a tool that fits any objective.

To make the process easier for beginners, Facebook allows users to choose their goal:

- Brand awareness vs. reach

- Traffic vs. engagement vs. lead generation

- Conversions vs. catalog sales vs. visits

Each type of consumer engagement campaign also has subtypes that will allow you to choose your engagement objective. These will allow you to gain more followers, attain more likes and shares on posts, and run an ad until a specific engagement goal is met.

Target Your Ideal Audience

Facebook has over one billion daily users who are basically customers just waiting to buy your products. Not just prospective customers are on Facebook; basically, *everyone* is.

This means CEOs, entrepreneurs, and people with deep pockets. No matter who your target audience is, they are on Facebook and most other social media platforms.

With all of this being said, simply posting on a Facebook page or profile isn't going to be good enough to turn social media users into buyers. Facebook ads are what will bring your business to the next level, but they have to be successful ads that generate sales.

If you're still a little unsure of who your audience is, don't take it to heart. You're new at this, and most people don't know how to reach a specific audience effectively. Facebook gives you three basic audience options: cold, warm, and customer.

A cold audience reach is basically sending out your ads to the entire Facebook universe and hoping something sticks. A warmer audience consists of people already connected to your page. Finally, a custom audience allows you to reach certain consumers who like specific pages or have specific interests. *This* is where your market research will come into play.

Selecting people who have already liked and followed your page will make it easier for you to convert them into customers. In addition, you are following up with people who are already familiar with your company and the products or services you're selling.

If you don't have that many followers to advertise to, but you have a customer list, designing a custom audience option may be the right path for you. You can upload your ideal audience list directly onto Facebook. The site will automatically generate a similar audience list made up of users who fit the description of the list you uploaded.

So what if you don't have any followers or a customer list? Believe it or not, this is one of the most common situations for new small businesses and startups.

For now, you'll have to use the "Everyone on Facebook" option when creating ads. The goal is to run a few ads and narrow your audience down to who you want your customers to be. Going from targeting the largest group of people possible to pruning the list down to only the ideal consumers can seem like a daunting task. The Facebook Audience Tool is really going to help a lot when going through the process.

Start by specifying the parameters of your ads and audience. Yes, it would be cool if you could make international sales, but it's best if you only advertise to people within the United States.

You will also want to choose the age group your ads are targeting. By setting up these two parameters, you already have a great foundation to grow your marketing campaigns.

Next, research what your competition is doing. Search for data about their followers. What are their interests? What celebrities do they follow? What draws their attention?

When it comes to selecting similar pages that reflect an audience pattern, this is the deciding factor of how well your ads do. Under the "interests" category, you can select individuals who like the pages that belong to your competition.

For argument's sake, let's pretend that you are opening up a local coffee house. This would make your greatest competition the bigger chains such as Starbucks or Dunkin Donuts.

Think about the target audience for Starbucks then apply the parameters of your target audience of 18 to 25-year-olds within the United States. The people in this category are college students and younger millennials who have very specific interests.

You can now select people to target your ads to by going through their pages and interests. Going back to the Audience Insight Tool, you can now provide greater demographic information for the people who follow those other companies.

Use Images that Pop and Catch the Eye

They say that a picture is worth a thousand words. When it comes to advertising, you're limited in how many words and images you can use to get your message across.

Once again, the age of technology has become the game changer in advertising and media consumption.

This means that the way you present your ads has to fit the method and platform you'll use to showcase them.

Almost everyone has a cell phone or tablet that allows them to scroll through social media sites, but the rate at which information is consumed is almost unfathomable.

Advertisements have to be even more eye-catching to attract a customer's attention immediately. You have to use bright colors, flashy images that are constantly changing, and say your business's message quickly.

If your ads are dull you risk taking too long to get the point across or don't touch on how your products can help fill some sort of need, then consumers will scroll right past your stuff.

One of the secrets to Facebook advertising is to use images that contain less than 20% of text or Facebook will display your ads to fewer members. You should use images that are relevant to your business and convey an ideal lifestyle to your target audience.

Let's say that I am targeting middle-aged married women who are housewives and fall into the middle class. I would show images of a woman similar to their image, enjoying an oil pen while lounging in the sun by the poolside. Wow, just thinking about it makes me want to fly out to the Bahamas and light up.

Even more effective than pictures are videos. Remember, you don't have to be a tech genius to produce some quality content. Heck, it would take you 30 minutes on YouTube learning simple editing techniques, and you're good to go!

Videos show a lot more information than just one image. Instagram and Facebook both have autoplay features, which will quickly snag your customer's attention. Rather than showing a still image that is easy to skip over.

Another helpful tip: create videos that don't rely on sound to get your message across.

This is for two reasons:

- People are impatient would rather quickly read or see what you have to offer and then continue scrolling

- Over 85% of videos on social media are watched on mute. Most people just simply don't keep their sound on.

The last word of advice I'll give you before moving onto my next point is to use images that are bright, clear, and feature people's faces.

Our brains are hardwired to recognize faces, so your ads will immediately catch attention.

Having people in your ads using your products will make them appear to be more relatable.

Know What to Say and How to Say It

"I still don't know how to write an ad, and I have no idea where to start!" This is what you may be thinking right now.

To be honest, I'm not the best at coming up with catchy phrases or using elegant words and knowing exactly how to get someone to buy from you.

I had to learn everything I know about marketing and figure out what works through trial and error.

I recently looked back through some of my old advertisement drafts, and they were truly not that great. But even if you're not great with words, there is a basic yet effective formula that will boost your marketing to the next level.

The most successful copy for social media ads contain three key elements:

- ➢ An attention grabber

- ➢ Value adder

- ➢ Call to action

The process behind this genius works like this:

- ➤ The first sentence is the attention grabber. It makes your customers stop and look at your ad.

- ➤ The second sentence drawers your reader in. It shows how your product or service adds value. It generates interest and keeps their attention.

- ➤ Finally, the last few sentences should be a call to action. It gets your readers to become customers and move on to buying your product or visiting your website or whatever else you want them to do.

Make sure that your call to action is clear and direct in order to achieve the maximum benefit from your ads. "Learn more" and "click to redeem now" are common call to action lines.

Keep in mind that the most successful Facebook ads contain buzzwords like *sale, limited time, free,* etc. Creating a sense of urgency is what will motivate potential customers more than anything else.

You can provide all the quality you want, but the basic principle of supply and demand rules above all. If you lead consumers to believe that your supply is running out, then they will flock to buy whatever you have left.

Your head is probably filling with great ad ideas and catch phrases to entice your customers with. You're gonna have to pump the brakes on whatever sales slogan you have running through your head.

Now that you know what to say to make your ads pop, you need to learn what *not* to say. Facebook and other social media sites have filtration systems that water down the appearance of advertisements that are too salesy.

For example, running too many ads with the words *you, money,* and *income* will raise red flags on your posts, which could even lead to your account being suspended. However, variations of those words will make your ads golden.

When it comes down to it, people don't like being advertised to. There have been multiple studies that have proven that consumers tend to reject any attempts to persuade them.

Even though this seems counterintuitive, the most successful ads that you can run don't actually sound like advertisements. You want customers to understand that it is in their best interest to click on your advertisements rather than just telling them to do it.

You've Run Your Ads, Now What?

Finally! It's time to start running your ads and making some real money. It is a rare occurrence for your ads to be successful on the first try.

Let's face it, even with the richest and wisest person coaching you failure is going to be part of the process. This is when A/B split testing your advertisements comes into play.

A/B split testing is when you have two or three slightly different ads running at the same time in order to determine what styles or wording are the most effective in converting observers to consumers.

You can then ideally create advertisements that combine the best elements of your old ads in order to sell better. A good place to start is changing the headlines and target audience.

Keep in mind that even though you want to run a few ads at once and keep trying new formulas with reaching different audiences, and the other hundred small details that go into creating marketing strategies, there is one important factor that you should never *ever* forget: money.

Social media sites are platforms that are motivated by money. Of course, they are businesses, and that's just how the world works. To put it plainly, the more money you're willing to spend, the more people will see your posts.

It is easy to get excited and go overboard with a dozen different ads. A healthy budget is what will keep you sane and stop you from breaking the bank.

Unfortunately, it is impossible for me to tell you what the average budget is for running social media ads. The money you allocate depends on variables like how expensive your weed is, how much you can manufacture, how big your target audience is, and how much you want to make within the next three, six, and twelve months.

Small businesses have stricter budgets than large companies. A one-man dispensary is different than a storefront that sells paraphernalia.

Another factor is that local ads will be cheaper than national ads. My advice is to start out with $5 a day towards advertisements then give more funding to ads that run better.

Keep Your Eye on the Competition

Even though the marijuana industry is still new, you're going to have competition. After all, great minds think alike, which is why you're reading this book right now.

Now that you know who your current customers are and what they are buying, it's time for you to check out the competition. Identifying who is interacting with your competitors can help answer some key questions about your own business.

- Is the competition targeting the same market segments that you are?

- Are they reaching new consumers that you hadn't considered before?

- How are they positioning their ads and shaping their brand image?

Although you won't be able to get detailed consumer research about the people connecting with your competitors, you will be able to get a general idea of their marketing strategy and whether it is allowing them to generate enough online engagement.

If their methods are effective, then you can adopt them into your own strategies in order to efficiently reach your target audience and beyond.

It doesn't matter what stage you are in with your business or how well your current ads are performing. You should always revisit your audience research as needed. When you go back through your research and experiment, you will come up with new ideas and ways to reach your audience.

You can also see new audience opportunities that may not have been there before. Think of it like reading the same book over and over again. Each time you read it, there are tiny details that you didn't notice before.

Use the information you learn from your failures and wins and revisit your target market statement on a regular basis to make sure that it incorporates the most valuable potential consumers.

Methods of Income for the Non-Salesman

Despite the political taboo surrounding marijuana use, the legality of the drug is the very least of users' cares as cannabis becomes more accessible.

In fact, in early 2018, Jeff Sessions, who served as Attorney General from 2017-2018, announced that the Justice Department was abolishing the guidelines that kept federal prosecutors from pursuing cannabis charges in states that legalized marijuana during the Obama-era.

Despite government scare tactics, the growing marijuana industry in the United States is only continuing to expand and welcome new users. Right after Session's declaration, a private equity firm announced a $100 billion project for seeking weed-related ventures.

As the industry continues to skyrocket, there are hundreds if not thousands of opportunities out there to make money off of this questionable plant.

In October 2018, a Gallup poll found that more than 60% of Americans are in favor of legalizing the drug. Experts estimate that annual sales of legal cannabis in North America will reach at least $22 billion by the year 2021.

That's a lot of weed.

As with any industry that is rapidly growing, legal cannabis offers many opportunities for investors to jump in at several entry points. Let's be honest; selling or growing weed isn't for everybody.

You've already seen in previous chapters just how many hoops you have to jump through in order to open a dispensary. It takes a certain person with the right amount of grit to power through the process of opening up a weed business.

From a personal standpoint, I can tell you just how exhausting it is to keep up with the changing regulations and federal laws that come into play. I didn't let that stop me from pursuing other avenues to make an income.

One of the greatest perks of being your own boss, whether it's full time or on the side, is that you can generate multiple streams of income and make as much money as you desire. There's no cap on how many businesses you can try or have, or how much income you can create.

You can grab some shares of cannabis producers or individuals who create marijuana-based products. You can get in on the ground floor of companies that offer services or products to the industry itself.

Keep reading to discover new legal ways to make money with marijuana, without actually selling it.

Branded Weed Products

This is where cannabis meets fashion and merchandising.

Legal marijuana doesn't have a lot of brand recognition. There is no singular string that is marketed as the "best," or "most refreshing," like the branding Apple and Pepsi promote.

One of the companies that are leading the way to break through this barrier is Cannabis Sativa Inc. Cannabis Sativa Inc. makes a variety of marijuana products, such as mints, edible, blams, etc. It even patented a strain of bud.

By using a business model similar to the retail locations of Apple, the company was able to build a brand whose mission is to help customers find reliable products in an industry that is easily flooded with untrustworthy weed and paraphernalia.

Being directly involved with marijuana products or plants isn't the only path you can take when it comes to building a brand around weed. Creating a website or online content are other avenues you can take to make money through cannabis.

For example, becoming a product reviewer, whether it's smoking weed, testing CBD products, or analyzing other companies to determine whether or not their products are legitimate can help build positive awareness around marijuana while also allowing you to make cash on the side.

When it comes to a niche as new and uncharted as weed, consumers are looking for people they can trust to point them in the right direction.

Why not become that person?

Investing

It doesn't matter how knowledgeable you are about a niche or how experienced you are in an industry; investing is a strong and legitimate way to increase your income.

The best part is that you don't necessarily have to hire a financial consultant or talk to several experts to learn how to invest. With the internet and unlimited access to books and videos created by those experts, you can learn the in's and out's of investing easily and without spending an obscene amount of money.

The cannabis business no longer an underground network now that legalization is coming to the forefront.

Instead, you can find companies that are involved with cannabis-related business listed on the major stock exchanges in the United States.

Several larger cannabis companies in the United States have been accumulating venture capital funds.

The first marijuana exchange traded fund (ETF) has four dozen stocks that are related to the marijuana industry.

Investing allows you to take advantage of the opportunity pot presents while still allowing you to keep some distance between you and Mary Jane.

It may seem obvious, but the more important part of investing is researching it as much as possible before diving in.

Make sure that the stocks you choose to invest in are legitimate and reputable cannabis companies.

A good place to start is researching the companies involved in the medical marijuana niche as you start getting a feel for the industry.

You can also think outside the box on this one and get really creative.

You can also look into organic fertilizer manufacturers, restaurants, and even cannabis friendly entertainment venues are all excellent places to start that don't include you being directly involved with the plant.

Another bonus with this approach is that you get to expand your portfolio while diversifying it.

Crypto Currencies

I know you've probably heard thousands of opinions and empty jabber about cryptos. When it comes to digital currencies, everyone has their two cents.

There is a ton of speculation about Bitcoin and Litecoin out there, but I can tell you that I personally have investments in cryptocurrencies and have made over $20,000 in two years. Not a bad deal for me, and I only originally invested $7,000.

Getting back to the main point, the cannabis industry is ignoring the hysteria and negative concerns over digital currencies and focusing on the way they can use the underlying blockchain technology.

For dispensaries that have been neglected and purposely overlooked by the traditional banking system, cryptos are the answer to a very prominent and serious issue within the industry.

As we all know, doing business only in cash is dangerous and leaves plenty of room for mistakes and misfortune.

Cryptos give businesses a fair chance to succeed and grow in ways that are otherwise impossible.

Take for instance, Budbo. This is a phone app that is designed to find cannabis products at local dispensaries. Budbo is working to include a blockchain-powered sales system for pot companies and has even created its own digital coin.

Getting Involved in Other Jobs Within the Market

The marijuana industry has created a ton of new jobs.

A report from the marijuana-based website Leafly actually found that the United States has approximately 211,000 full-time legal marijuana jobs, with more than 64,000 added in 2018.

There are a variety of positions out there. Find the right one for your schedule that will still allow you to make a significant side income. Just like applying for any other job, marketing yourself and highlighting the right skill set will allow you to excel in the job market.

One example of a career that came from the marijuana industry is Canada's national health department quality control analyst positions. These jobs have an average national salary of $72,000. It's safe to say that jobs involved in the marijuana sector that are similar to those already established pay almost double.

The simplest way to start is looking for a dispensary job. Sometimes owning a shop, investing, or being a property manager isn't within your interests, so working at a dispensary might be the direction you're looking for.

If being a counter clerk, security agent, or weed connoisseur isn't what you want to do, you can find a cannabis-based career with Hemp Staff and other similar services. They post job listings that fall within the industry and show you opportunities to receive training to work in the industry.

A few additional examples of jobs within the weed market are:

> ➤ Budtenders who are similar to bartenders, but instead of serving alcohol, you are an expert in finding the perfect strain for each customer's needs.
>
> ➤ Delivery drivers for medicinal cannabis dispensaries
>
> ➤ Master growers who manage teams of growers and growing rooms

If this is the route that you're going to take, make sure that you connect with legal operations that have been legitimized.

Real Estate Opportunities

In states that have legalized marijuana, major cities are experiencing incredible population growth and real estate booms. In other words, this is amazing news if you're looking to invest in real estate where cannabis is dispensed legally.

Buying and managing apartment buildings in a legal marijuana neighborhood may be one of the greatest long-term investment opportunities available. In cities where new dispensaries or cannabis farms pop up, housing will become a premium investment.

Getting into the real estate game now will put you ahead of the game. If working or managing long-term renters isn't ideal for you, then short-term renting is another option that can be just as lucrative.

Listing a home or apartment for rent on websites like Bud and Breakfast can help connect you with people who are interested in staying at your weed-friendly place.

Outdoor Grow Operations

Land is hardly ever a bad investment no matter what market you're looking to break into. Of course, you want to be responsible with your research when purchasing any parcel of land, whether it's a house, farm, or storefront.

As I'm sure you can imagine by the pages of policies and laws from previous chapters, we're talking about land in states that have legalized or decriminalized weed.

For example, in the state of Washington, outdoor cannabis growing facilities must be enclosed by a wall or fence that is at least eight feet tall. Meanwhile, in the state of Colorado, growers are completely prohibited from moving their operations outside, no matter how secure the facilities are.

If growing pot plants outside sounds like the first step you want to take in your marijuana business, the Pacific Northwest is the ideal region to found your company. The climate makes cannabis easy to maintain, making it one of the most financially lucrative crops you can farm.

The roots of the plants themselves can expand at an exponential rate growing rapidly to produce more bud to pick and sell. Growing outdoors also allows your plants to reach ten feet or higher in growth, as they aren't inhibited by the ceiling or artificial light.

When it comes down to comparing product, the proof is in the taste and feel of the bud. The fact of the matter is that pristine, quality weed cannot always be achieved through indoor growth.

After all, Mary Jane is a product of Mother Nature so who better to grow it than the expert herself? While you may still have to conduct routine maintenance on your plants, nature will do the majority of the work.

Growing Facilities

The other and arguably more lucrative investment in real estate is funding your own growing operation. This may seem like a big risk in the shadow of national laws and regulations, but it can be done successfully if curated correctly.

It starts with choosing a grow site. Just like shopping for a retail storefront, searching for a production facility that serves the needs and purposes of your business plays a key role in how consumers will measure the credibility of your business.

For instance, ensuring that the location provides the space and environment that can be manipulated so that your plants can mature rapidly and you can expand as needed.

Owning or renting a growing facility comes with other benefits that can't be found in using a storefront for other operations, such as dispensaries. Choosing an out-of-the-way location to host your plants offers greater security, expansion opportunities, and logistics.

There are already restrictions in place in certain states that inhibit producers from opening grow businesses too close to schools, transit centers, parks, libraries, and other buildings that cater to minors.

Space, Ventilation, and Air

Indoor cannabis operations need to be in an enclosed and absolutely secure building, with windows, walls, doors, and a roof that function properly. While it may seem that any old warehouse will do for hosting your plants, you need to think about the true worth of weed in this day and age.

Cannabis is in constantly high demand, with the black market still coming out as the true monopoly in the industry. However, your greatest competition will be with the plants themselves.

Operating a successful commercial marijuana grow business is expensive and challenging. It all comes down to the science of growing.

I could write an entire second book on the science, methods, and mechanics of growing weed. There really is *that* much information on the subject. My point is that you have to do your research and consume as much information as possible if this is the route that you decide to take.

As a grower, you need to consistently control the humidity, light, and environment surrounding the plants.

For me, growing my own product was the next step in my business plan. It gave me more control over my income and allowed me to understand cannabis on a whole new level.

The lighting, temperature, and energy use within your growing facilities will be your top priorities in marijuana production.

The first thing you need to look for when searching for your commercial grow location is space.

These plants can grow over ten feet tall, and you need to be able to give them the space necessary to produce bud.

Of course, you can start small with a few plants inside a 5 x 10 foot grow tent, but you'll want to think bigger as an entrepreneur.

In any industry, whether it's food, hospitality, or botany, customers want consistent quality. This can only be delivered through the finest grow operations.

The next item on your facility checklist will be ventilation. A potential grow space requires ventilation for your plant and a lot of light to ensure proper ventilation and air exchange. As a grower, you risk cooking your crop or limiting how much bud they produce through excess heat, oxygen, and humidity.

Are you feeling overwhelmed yet? Well, don't. There are greenhouse-specific HVAC systems that will help you accurately maintain the climate of your space without putting your plants at risk.

When it comes to potting your plants, each individual plant should have its own 5-gallon pot. Like I said before, these plants grow quickly, and their roots expand much faster than most other plants.

They require a lot of room or else your crop will be small and significantly lower in quality. After buying the right pots for your pot, you need to choose the right soil.

Anyone with even the smallest background in botany knows that the type of soil you treat your plants with will give them the right nutrients to thrive. After potting your plants, you need to carefully monitor the pH levels of the soil to ensure that it falls between 5.5 to 6.5, which is the preferred level for cannabis.

Let There Be Light!

Light: the photo in photosynthesis. No, I'm obviously not a scientist, but I can tell you that your plants will need precise lighting to reach their potential.

Obviously, sunlight and water are two non-negotiables for growing. Costs of electricity will be your top expense for your grow facility, typically more than your other costs *combined*.

Dehumidifiers, ventilation, air conditioning, and lighting will require an insane amount of electricity. What's a guy to do other than look for ways to cut down these costs?

This is where energy efficiency comes into play without having to sacrifice the quality of your product. There is much debate when it comes to using artificial lighting for marijuana greenhouses because natural light is always the ideal solution. However, several studies have demonstrated that High-

Pressure Sodium (HPS) lights provide more consistency for indoor growing.

As an entrepreneur, you can't overlook energy efficiency standards within the initial construction of your facility.

Here's an example to put this idea into perspective. Approximately 2% of Denver, Colorado's annual energy usage in 2014 went towards cannabis grow facilities.

Even with only a handful of states legalizing cannabis, an estimated 1% of the nation's energy usage, equating to about six billion dollars, goes towards grow operations.

So, what are your options when it comes to saving energy and money? In my experience, there are three routes you can take.

Investing in Solar Energy

It's not a secret that solar energy is slowing becoming more affordable, especially when it is purchased and installed in larger scales.

Many agree that it is due to the legalized state of Colorado investing in solar power for their grow houses that has lead to the greater availability of solar panels. The state is expecting that by 2020, it will generate over 30% of its electricity from renewable and reusable energy sources.

Just as innovators and moguls have predicted, marijuana legalization is sparking creativity, new technology, and large scale adoption of energy efficient solutions across the globe.

Reuse and Recycle Water

It may not seem like water will be a significant expense because it's something we hardly ever think about. Running a business that requires a considerable amount of water at the cost of your plants will run your water bill higher than you'd think.

In the United Kingdom's brewing industry, cannabis growers are investing in closed-circuit desalination (CCD), also known as reverse osmosis water systems. While still purifying incoming community water sources, CCD technology can recover over 90% of wastewater. This inherently reduces water demand and saves you a ton of money in disposal fees.

Smaller operations in rainy climates, such as Washington state, are putting their funding towards rainwater collection and storage to save on the cost of irrigation.

You might be thinking, "this doesn't affect me, I won't have more than a few plants at most. And this information is for someone who wants to be on the same scale as a drug lord." I thought the same thing when I first invested in my own plants.

Did you know that just *one* cannabis plant uses as much as 22 liters of water in a day? *That's* the reality of how much you'll be saving by switching to a cost-effective water retention system.

If you're not planning on transplanting your operation to the North Pacific, then you'll have to confront the issue of lower precipitation that outdoor growing ultimately features.

Designing Your Own Greenhouse

According to a 2018 article in a Denver based magazine, growers who choose to utilize an energy efficient greenhouse pay less than half the costs of producers who grow their plants in a warehouse environment.

Setting up a business in an already risky marketplace means that you have to be careful where you invest your money. Taking extra precautions when it comes down to the operations of your business is only going to benefit you in the long run.

It is important to choose a functional and sustainable facility to grow your plants during the beginning stages of your business to make scaling optimizable in the future.

A 2016 article by Entrepreneur Magazine found a correlation between producing in a sustainable facility and profit markings on large scale operations. This means that bigger growing businesses and distributors would be in a more beneficial market position if the United States decides to legalize cannabis on a national scale.

As the industry continues to gain traction, private investors have begun funding research for the most affordable and efficient methods of growing, so that the best and most valuable systems are utilized to optimize production.

Security and Compliance for Growing

The cannabis market is expected to reach an estimated $20-30 billion within the next few years. This means that security and compliance with your state's regulations is absolutely essential to your success in the recreational weed industry.

Your prosperity in the cannabis world relies on the account for your highly valuable cash crop, the cash-only basis of the business, and the state level regulations and restrictions on your production and sale of the product.

You also need to make sure that you hire employees that you can trust with your business who will be discreet about your operations.

It is crucial that you invest in extensive and advanced weed security solutions, regardless of how small your venture is here in the beginning stages.

In the end, once again, state laws are king when it comes to compliance and structure.

It is essential that you thoroughly research where you want your operation to be and how to adhere to that state's laws.

For example, in the state of Washington, you must provide:

- Identification and photographs to confirm your identity

- Identification badges for any visitors who are not employees or customers of your business.

- A security system equipped with an alarm for all entry points and windows.

- An updated surveillance system that has a separate storage device that records up to forty- five days of storage, as well as internet protocol that also meets the state's requirements.

- A tracking system that records the seed to sale process.

Promoting Cannabis-based Products

Still think that selling, producing, or transporting cannabis products aren't your path into the marketplace? Then look no further than the products that already exist.

In this new world of decriminalized drugs, people who are new to the marijuana culture and industry are looking to knowledgeable and experienced guides to help them through this new world of information.

Choosing and promoting cannabis products may just be the right path for you, especially if you currently reside in a country or state that has already legalized weed.

There are a plethora of ways that you can legally get high-quality cannabis products and seeds.

The premise of your business is strongly founded on your ability to consider which strains to choose and how your recommendations match other people's needs through the sources that are available to consumers.

There is one flaw in the realm of product sponsorship. When it comes to strain-specific data, the research is, for the most part, nonexistent.

Noone has been able to gather consumer data on strains that are bestsellers, seasonal changes, and the long term studies of cannabis use and effects.

This type of shift in the political and economic climate is nearly unprecedented, only to be compared to the prohibition of the 1920s.

Without data to guide your promotions or contribute credibility to your presence, you're basically starting from ground zero in building your customer base.

Regardless of the lack of data and research, you are still expected to have a wide range of knowledge on almost all products, strains, and paraphernalia within the industry.

Even though there is no way to know which strains would sell the best at this moment, there are vast differences between strains in where and how they grow, taste, smell, and affect your high.

The ability to tell your viewers or customers which products are legitimate will absolutely add to your status as an influencer in the market.

Believe it or not, many products are incorrectly classified when it comes to strains and effectiveness.

Think of all the "fitness influencers" on social media today. Imagine the incredible success of the people who first got into the market and created the paths for the thousands of newer profiles that now flood Instagram, Facebook, and Twitter.

The industry may be small right now, but in a few years it will be booming.

You'll have wished that you started promoting products sooner because customers will appreciate and value the longevity of your presence.

Funding and Financing in Cannabis Ventures

Surprise! Another word on the bottom line: the money.

I may be beating a dead horse here, but I wanted to quickly cover a bit more of the financial aspect of funding a cannabis business especially when you aren't directly involved in the selling of the plant.

Unfortunately, major financial institutions are not going to start lending money to individuals who want to start their own marijuana based company. This is because FDIC insurance rules state that banks can lose their federal protection if they invest in existential risks such as companies who are challenging federal law.

Now more than ever, private financial institutions are starting to take on marijuana companies who support and serve growers and retailers but who aren't involved with the plants or bud directly.

If you need more money for your start-up, look towards venture capital, angel investors, private equity funding, and private lenders for a leg up.

To get you started, here are a few conditions and requirements that will help you secure financial backing:

- ➤ Become a corporation

- ➤ Create and maintain a business bank account

- ➤ Have at least six months of strong operations

- ➤ Make monthly gross sales of at least $10,000

- ➤ Maintain a credit score over 500

Conclusion

This is it! You're almost ready to go out and make your mark on the world in a way that others only dream of.

Running your own business isn't a piece of cake, but I can guarantee that this last word of advice will solidify your startup and propel you into this venture with confidence.

When is started my own small business, my goal wasn't to get rich quick or become a millionaire in five years. I started it because I saw a need in a market that was somewhat familiar and wanted to work as hard as I could to make it happen because I *knew* that it would work.

I didn't imagine that I would quit my day job to pursue it full-time or that I would be writing this book. The most successful people that you can think of in today's world don't dream of making millions but of making a lasting impact for the people who are within their niche.

If you think that this is a shortcut into entrepreneurship, then you're wrong. It takes hard work, commitment, and a winner's attitude to start a business and make it grow into something incredible.

If this is the path you choose, then don't let anyone stop you from going after your goals. I can't tell you how many people said I was crazy or that this country would never let an industry like this succeed.

I kept working and pushing forward. Today I couldn't be happier with the results. Trust your own instincts and learn as much as you can about this market, because the payout does come.

Lastly, thank you for reading this book. This opportunity to be someone that others can look up to and use as a guide is so great, and I only wish you the best on this exciting new adventure. It will be hard, but I promise that it will be worth it.

If this book has inspired you in any way, would you please consider leaving a review wherever you purchased this book? I value your feedback, and I look forward to reading your comments.